THE
WHAT, WHEN AND WHERE GUIDE
TO NORTHERN CALIFORNIA

The

What, When and Where Guide

to Northern California

by
Basil Charles Wood

Doubleday & Company, Inc.
Garden City, New York
1977

Library of Congress Cataloging in Publication Data

Wood, Basil Charles.
　　The what, when, and where guide to northern California.

　　Includes index.
　　　1.　California—Description and travel—1951-
—Guide-books.　I.　Title.
F859.3.W66　　　917.94'04'5

To Doris, whose constant encouragement,
advice and sound practical help has made this book possible.
Without her, it just wouldn't exist.

NORTHERN CALIFORNIA

AREA MAP

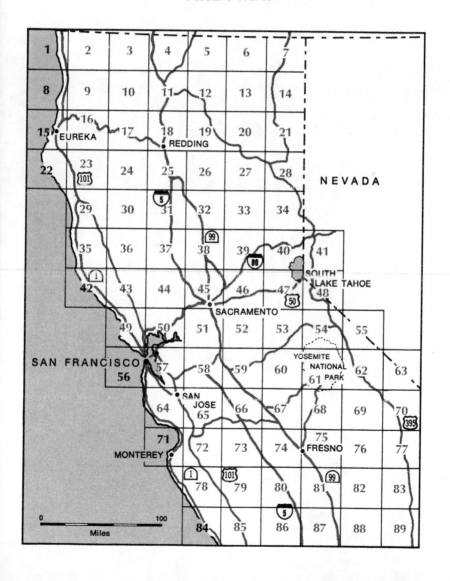

CONTENTS

How to use this guide _____ xvii

Places to visit

AMUSEMENT PARKS

CHILDREN'S PLAYGROUNDS

NARROW GAUGE RAILROADS

ZOOS

OBSERVATORIES & PLANETARIUMS

FERRIES, RIVER & BAY CRUISES

ART GALLERIES & ART EXHIBITS

ART GALLERIES & ART EXHIBITS

MUSEUMS & EXHIBITS

MUSEUMS & EXHIBITS

MUSEUMS & EXHIBITS

MISSIONS & PLACES OF WORSHIP

STATE & COUNTY PARKS & HISTORIC LANDMARKS

xiii

HOMES & BUILDINGS OF HISTORIC INTEREST

NATIONAL PARKS & MONUMENTS

BOTANICAL GARDENS & NATURE CENTERS

PARKS

MISCELLANEOUS

MISCELLANEOUS

MISCELLANEOUS

WINERIES

SCENIC CHAIR RIDES

WINERIES

INDUSTRIAL TOURS

HOW TO USE THIS GUIDE

If you have ever squinted through pages of small type to find out when a museum will be open, you will understand the reason for this guide. If you are a parent who has wrestled with an unwieldy road map in one hand and an oversized tourist book in the other—while the rest of the family cries, "How much farther?"—you will find this guide a soothing antidote for travel headaches, eyestrain, heartburn and, perhaps best of all, an overextended budget.

This is a quick-reference guide, designed for everyone who wants to know at a glance WHAT there is to see . . . WHEN it's open . . . HOW MUCH it costs . . . and WHERE it can be reached by the simplest route.

How This Guide Can Save You Money

Use this guide in planning your trips by combining visits to several attractions that are all located in the same vicinity. Admission costs are clearly listed—many interesting places are free—so you can easily determine the amount you wish to spend and how far you want to travel without danger of getting lost or going over the top of your budget.

Northern California, an area stretching from San Simeon to the Oregon border, encompasses some of the most magnificent country in the state. Rich in history and scenic beauty, it has countless places to explore, or simply to view with awe. Among them are the majestic Yosemite valley and sparkling Lake Tahoe; mining towns where the ghosts of the '49ers still seem to lurk in the shadows of decaying buildings; numerous museums, both traditional and unusual; towering redwood forests with some of the oldest and biggest trees in the world; exciting narrow-gauge railroads and adventuresome river trips, vineyards ripening in the sun. Northern California indeed has it all. And on top of that, it has San Francisco.

So many interesting places to visit, so many things to do . . . but unless you know exactly where they are, it's easy to drive within a mile or so of one of them and miss it just because you didn't realize how close you were!

This book has individual maps specially designed to accompany each subject, and also to show the location of other attractions nearby. When touring the state you can plan your route to include visits to several of these places at once, thereby avoiding unnecessary travel and saving costly gas.

Tips on How to Use the Guide

The Table of Contents groups all attractions under major headings—Amusement Parks, Zoos, Museums, Art Galleries, etc. If you should like to visit the Mission San Carlos Borremeo (The Carmel Mission), for example, you will find it listed under "Missions & Places of Worship." To the *left* will be a column headed "Area Number" and opposite the mission is the number 71. Now turn to the Area Map in the very front of this guide and you will see it is divided by a grid into numbered areas. This enables you to locate any attraction in relation to the whole of Northern California. Carmel Mission is in area 71, near Monterey on the California coastline.

Opposite The Carmel Mission in the Table of Contents on the *right* hand side is a page number, in this case 2. Turn to page 2 and you will find the mission described and a clear map showing you how to get there. On the same map you will see that the very beautiful Point Lobos State Reserve is close by and well worth a visit. Adjoining the map on the same page are all the pertinent details you need to know, such as opening hours and cost of admission.

Wineries

While you are touring this northern part of the state, take the opportunity to visit one or more of its many wineries. California produces some of the finest premium and table wines, and a visit to the wine-making areas can be a most interesting and enjoyable experience. A list of those wineries whose facilities are open to the public is given on page 126.

Industrial Tours

An added feature of this book is its listing of various industrial tours. It's fun to see how the things we use every day are made, operated, grown or packaged—and educational too. Many companies offer tours of their facilities, and a selected list is included, beginning on page 134. Not all tours are of interest to young children. Some companies specify age limits and also limit the number of persons per tour. Nearly all require reservations, so please be sure to telephone or write first (numbers and addresses are given in the Industrial Tour Section).

The Guide as Your Traveling Companion

Your *What, When and Where Guide to Northern California* packs a great deal into its 139 pages but, of course, cannot be all-inclusive. It is not a restaurant guide, for instance; there are plenty of those. It does not include all state parks or historic monuments but concentrates on places of widest general interest located within those parks.

Opening and closing times may be affected by national or state holidays, and it is usually advisable to telephone before planning to visit on a holiday. Daylight saving changes may also cause an adjustment in the hours of operation. The hours listed were in effect when we went to press, as were the costs of admission.

Frequently used, kept around the house or in the glove compartment of your car, this guide will greatly stimulate and expedite your enjoyment of one of the world's most richly varied playgrounds. All information has been checked against data supplied by the attraction managements, for which we are grateful, and it is my hope that you will find this book to be enormously useful as you explore the wonders of Northern California.

–Basil Charles Wood

THE
WHAT, WHEN AND WHERE GUIDE
TO NORTHERN CALIFORNIA

POINT LOBOS STATE RESERVE Rte. 1 South of **Carmel** (408) 624-4909	This beautiful area covers 1,250 acres along the south shore of Carmel Bay, a naturalist's paradise with a magnificent stand of Monterey cypress, flowers, shrubs and many specimens of wildlife. Offshore, Sea Lion Rocks is the home of large colonies of seals and sea lions. During November the great California whale starts to migrate southward and can often be seen traveling close to shore.
MISSION SAN CARLOS BORROMEO (The Carmel Mission) Rio Rd. **Carmel** (408) 624-3600	The Carmel Mission was originally founded by Padre Junipero Serra in Monterey, but lack of good soil and its proximity to the Presidio resulted in re-establishment in its present location in Carmel. The mission was Father Serra's headquarters and home until his death on August 28, 1784. He is buried beneath the church floor in front of the chancel.
MISSION NUESTRA SENORA DE LA SOLEDAD **Soledad**	Unlike the other missions, Soledad, thirteenth in the chain, suffered greatly from neglect. Damage caused by floods in 1828 went unrepaired and eventually La Soledad ceased to exist as an operating mission. The land annd crumbling buildings were sold by Governor Pico for $800. Restoration of the chapel has now been completed by the Native Daughters of the Golden West and further restorative work continues.
MISSION SAN ANTONIO DE PADUA Hunter Liggett Military Hwy. **Jolon** (408) 385-4478	Father Junipero Serra chose a beautiful oak-dotted valley as the site of his third mission, which he dedicated on July 14, 1771. The site was changed to a place farther up Los Robles Valley two years later, and in 1810 the final church structure was started; the same building that stands reconstructed today. The grist mill, water wheel, wine vat and aqueduct system are among the many features of interest.

Daily,
9 am to 6 pm
Open to 8 pm in summer

$1.00 per car

Daily,

Mon. through Sat.
9:30 am to 5 pm

Sun. 11:30 am to 5 pm

Voluntary contributions

Daily, except Mon.
10 am to 4 pm

Free

Daily,
9:30 am to 5 pm

Donation

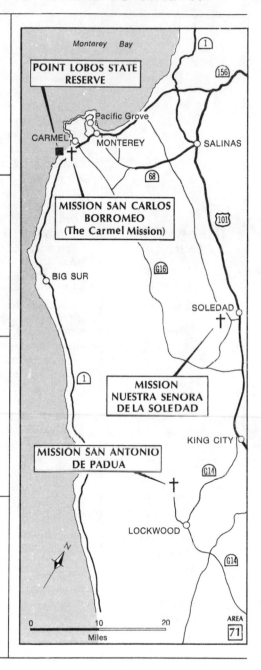

POINT LOBOS STATE RESERVE

MISSION SAN CARLOS BORROMEO (The Carmel Mission)

MISSION NUESTRA SENORA DE LA SOLEDAD

MISSION SAN ANTONIO DE PADUA

Monterey Bay

Pacific Grove

CARMEL

MONTEREY

SALINAS

BIG SUR

SOLEDAD

KING CITY

LOCKWOOD

0   10   20
Miles

AREA
71

3

THE MONTEREY PENINSULA

Monterey
and Carmel

White sandy beaches, pounding surf, craggy rocks and wind-swept cypresses and pines combine to make this area one of the most beautiful stretches of shoreline on the northern California coast.

Monterey is rich in history and many early-day buildings have been well preserved and are open to the public. Cannery Row, made famous in John Steinbeck's novel, has changed radically over the years, and the sardine factories have been replaced by galleries and fine restaurants.

Nearby, Carmel is a delightful village of small shops offering the widest variety of arts and craftwork, much of it of local origin but well augmented by imports from countries throughout the world. Many shops specialize in fine casual clothing for both men and women and, in general, Carmel is a tourist's shopping paradise.

Seventeen Mile Drive is a particularly beautiful scenic route from Carmel to Pacific Grove, including such points of interest as Seal Rock, the famed Cypress Point and also the golf courses that are the scene of the Crosby Pro-Am Tournament each spring. There is a toll of $3.00 for cars.

ALLEN KNIGHT MARITIME MUSEUM

550 Calle
Principal

(408) 375-2553

The days of sail, of fishing and whaling, and local naval history are depicted through a comprehensive collection of pictures, models and maritime artifacts.

Models of sail and steamships are well presented, including the frigate *Savannah*, flagship of Commodore John Drake Sloat, who seized Monterey in 1846. Many photographs, paintings and lithographs are also on view.

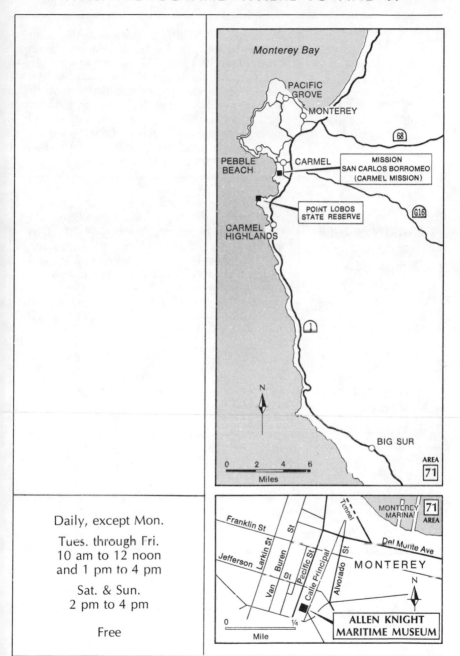

Daily, except Mon.

Tues. through Fri.
10 am to 12 noon
and 1 pm to 4 pm

Sat. & Sun.
2 pm to 4 pm

Free

COLTON HALL Dutra & King Sts. (408) 373-2103	The Reverend Walter Colton, first American *alcade* (mayor) and a naval chaplain, built Colton Hall in 1848. The following year the first Constitution of California was written there in both Spanish and English. The meeting room on the upper floor is furnished as it was at the signing of the Constitution and includes portraits of each of the participants. Behind the hall is the old Monterey Jail, open to visitors daily until 4:30 pm.
LARKIN HOUSE Calle Principal & Jefferson Street (408) 373-2103	The Larkin House was built in 1835 and is a combination of New England and Spanish Colonial architecture. From 1844 to 1846 the house served as the American Consulate. Of considerable architectural and historical interest, it contains many of the original furnishings. Tours last 35 minutes, the first leaving at 10 am and the last at 4:30 pm.
STEVENSON HOUSE 530 Houston Street (408) 373-2103	Named for Robert Louis Stevenson, this is the old boarding house where the famed author spent the latter months of 1879. The building dates back to 1830 and has been well restored. Several rooms have been devoted to the memory of Stevenson and are filled with artifacts and memorabilia.
U.S. ARMY MUSEUM The Presidio of Monterey **Monterey** (408) 242-8547	The museum houses an exhibition of relics, memorabilia and models that trace the history of the old Spanish Presidio on Lake El Estero, Monterey (founded in 1770), to the present "Old Fort Hill." In addition to three dioramas, exhibits range from early Spanish days through the colorful period of the U.S. Cavalry to World Wars I and II.

Daily,
10 am to 5 pm

Free

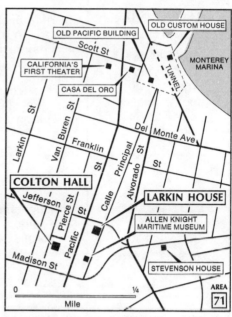

Daily, except Tues.
10 am to 4 pm
Guided tours only

Adults: 25¢
Under 19 free

Daily,
9 am to 4 pm
Tours on the hour,
every hour

Free

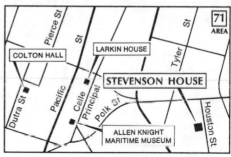

Wed. through Fri.
11 am to 1 pm
and 2 pm to 5 pm

Sat. & Sun.
10 am to 1 pm
and 2 pm to 5 pm

Free

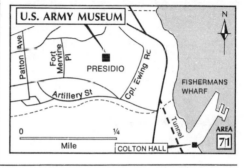

CALIFORNIA'S FIRST THEATER Pacific & Scott Sts. (408) 375-4916 for information on current presentations	In 1846 the building was a lodging house for sailors. In an effort to provide some sort of entertainment, a stage play was presented in 1847 and a small admission fee charged, thus the building became the first in California to charge admission for a theatrical performance. During the year old time plays are presented by artists of the Monterey Peninsula.
CASA DEL ORO Scott & Olivier Sts. (408) 373-2103	Now a State Historical Monument, this old building was originally a trading store, although through the years it has also served as a saloon and private residence. During gold-rush days it was used as a depository where miners could store their fortunes. Today it offers visitors a glimpse of history while they look at a fully equipped general store as it was a century ago.
OLD PACIFIC BUILDING Calle Principal &˜Scott St. (408) 373-2103	The building, constructed in 1847, was first rented to the U.S. Quartermaster to use for offices and storage. During later years it served in a variety of capacities, which included a tavern, newspaper, courtroom, boardinghouse and law office. It is now an excellent museum of California history, and on the upper floor there is featured an outstanding collection of Indian artifacts.
OLD CUSTOM HOUSE Custom House Plaza (408) 373-2103	This is the oldest government building in California and was built about 1827. It has flown the flags of Spain, Mexico and the United States, and in 1846, with the raising of the American flag here over Monterey, more than half a million square miles of territory became part of the United States. Pictures, flags, manuscripts and other historical items are on display in the museum.

Daily, except Mon.
9 am to 5 pm

Adults: 25¢
Children free

Daily,
10 am to 5 pm

Free

Daily,
9 am to 5 pm

Adults: 25¢
Under 18 free

Daily,
10 am to 5 pm

Free

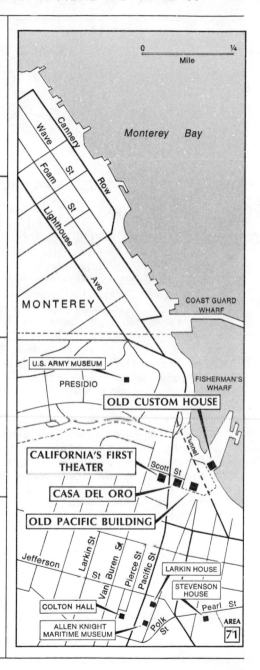

THE SANTA CRUZ AREA

Located at the north end of Monterey Bay and at the mouth of the San Lorenzo River, the city of Santa Cruz provides an excellent base from which to explore the many and varied attractions that are to be found in the surrounding area.

The Santa Cruz Playland is one of the last of the old-time ocean-side boardwalks, abounding with attractions and rides in a carnival-like atmosphere where something can be found to please every member of the family. A giant roller coaster, Ferris wheel, merry-go-round and other exciting rides share the boardwalk with a penny arcade and stalls selling cotton candy, candied apples and hot dogs. There are also snack bars and sit-down restaurants.

The public beach is one of the finest in northern California, well sheltered and, when the tide is out, offers exciting areas for exploration among the many tide pools.

Three miles to the west of Santa Cruz, Natural Bridges Beach State Park has excellent swimming and surf fishing. There is also a picnicking park. The gracefully arched natural bridges, which give the beach its name, have been formed by the incessant pounding and scouring action of ocean waves beating against the sandstone and are a favorite subject for photographers and artists.

VISITING SANTA CRUZ

Inland lies the Big Basin Redwoods State Park, which every visitor to Santa Cruz should endeavor to include in her or his itinerary. This beautiful area has one of the most frequently visited forests in California and, in 1902, was the first preserve of redwoods to be set aside as a state park. It contains some magnificent stands of giant trees, and also offers picnic sites, campgrounds (reservations required), small streams and more than 30 miles of hiking trials. During the summer months a planned recreation program includes guided nature hikes and a campfire program.

Near the city is the spectacularly scenic campus of the University of California at Santa Cruz. Set amid the redwoods, it presents magnificent ocean views from much of the campus area and is well worth a visit.

MYSTERY SPOT 1953 Branciforte Dr. **Santa Cruz** (408) 423-8897	The accepted laws of gravity do not appear to apply to this strange, puzzling part of a redwood forest where even the trees do not seem to grow up straight. Guided tours are given and the various phenomena demonstrated to puzzled visitors leaning backward or forward when they should be standing straight up, or finding that a companion has suddenly grown or shrunk.
MISSION SANTA CRUZ High St. **Santa Cruz** (408) 426-5686	Today a half-scale replica of the church stands not far from the original site where the mission was founded in 1791. Santa Cruz was the twelfth in the chain of California missions, and its location, amid fertile lands where Indians were friendly, held promise for much success. Unfortunately, floods and earthquakes gradually destroyed the buildings until finally no trace of the mission remained.
"THE LAST SUPPER" Santa Cruz Art League Galleries 526 Broadway **Santa Cruz** (408) 426-5787	"The Last Supper" is a remarkable, life-sized, wax figure interpretation of Leonardo Da Vinci's famous painting. The figures were sculptured by Katherine Stubergh and her daughter, who spent many months of painstaking research before commencing the project. A 10-minute narration is given at regular intervals. There is seating for 35 persons: reservations are not necessary.
THE MUSEUM OF NATURAL HISTORY 165 Forest Ave. **Pacific Grove** (408) 372-4212	A very comprehensive collection of exhibits relating to the natural history of the Monterey area makes a visit to this museum well worthwhile. On view is a wide array of California and tropical butterflies, stuffed models of sea otters, mammals, rodents and other indigenous creatures. A relief map depicts the geology of Monterey Bay together with exhibits of minerals, ore and fossils.

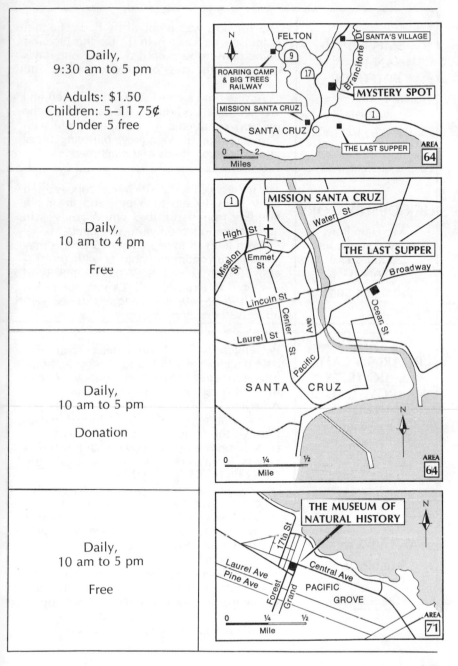

Daily,
9:30 am to 5 pm

Adults: $1.50
Children: 5–11 75¢
Under 5 free

N

FELTON
SANTA'S VILLAGE

ROARING CAMP
& BIG TREES
RAILWAY

9

17

MYSTERY SPOT

MISSION SANTA CRUZ

1

SANTA CRUZ

THE LAST SUPPER

0 1 2
Miles

AREA
64

Daily,
10 am to 4 pm

Free

1

MISSION SANTA CRUZ

High St

Water St

THE LAST SUPPER

Mission St

Emmet St

Broadway

Lincoln St

Center St

Ocean St

Laurel St

Pacific Ave

SANTA   CRUZ

N

0   ¼   ½
Mile

AREA
64

Daily,
10 am to 5 pm

Donation

Daily,
10 am to 5 pm

Free

THE MUSEUM OF
NATURAL HISTORY

N

17th St

Laurel Ave

Central Ave

Pine Ave

Forest

Grand

PACIFIC

GROVE

0   ¼   ½
Mile

AREA
71

MISSION SAN JUAN BAUTISTA State Historic Park **Bautista** (408) 623-4881	The mission was founded by Padre Fermin Francisco de Lasuen in 1797; the location being chosen because it was only one day's walk from the missions at Santa Clara and Carmel. At one time some 1,200 Indians lived and worked here, and during the early 1800s the mission conducted a flourishing trade with Yankee ships at Monterey, bartering hides and tallow for goods and machinery.
LICK OBSERVATORY Mt. Hamilton Hwy. 130, about 20 miles east of **SAN JOSE** (408) 274-5061	The gallery of the 120-inch telescope is open daily from 10 am to 5 pm, and the main building from 1 pm to 5 pm. A guide is in attendance (once only) on weekends. From June 15 to September 15 visitors may observe astronomical objects with the 12- and 36-inch refractors. Write for tickets to Visitors' Program, Lick Observatory, Mt. Hamilton 95140, enclosing a stamped self-addressed envelope.
ROARING CAMP & BIG TREES NARROW-GAUGE RAILROAD Graham Hill Rd. **Felton** (408) 335-4484	Passengers board colorful steam trains that date back to the 1880s and '90s for an hour-long excursion to Bear Mountain over one of the steepest railroad grades in North America. The entire route of the railroad passes through the famous Welch Big Trees Grove of redwoods and passengers have magnificent panoramas of the foret as the steam train chugs on its way.
SANTA'S VILLAGE State Route 17 **Santa Cruz** (408) 438-2250	A fairy-tale wonderland for children, Santa's Village is complete with such delights as a bobsled ride, reindeer-pulled sleigh and a giant snowball. Santa greets visitors to his year-round home where there are train rides, horseless carriages, a piano-playing duck, puppet shows, dancing chickens and other "educated" animals providing fun for every age.

14

Daily,
8 am to 5 pm

Adults: 25¢
Children free

Daily,
10 am to 5 pm

Free

Daily,
Summer: every hour,
11 am to 4 pm
Rest of year: daily at
12 noon with additional
services on weekends

Adults: $4.40
Children: 3–15 $2.45
Under 3 free

Daily,

mid-June through Labor Day
11 am to 5 pm,
Nov.–Dec.: 10 am to 5 pm
Rest of year:
school holidays & weekends
only.
Adults: $1.75 Children: 4–16
75¢
Under 4 free (Rides not included in
price of admission)

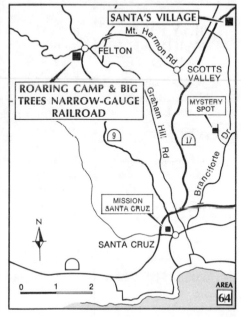

VILLA MONTALVO CENTER FOR THE ARTS & ARBORETUM Montalvo Rd. off Saratoga Los Gatos Rd., Hwy. 9 **Saratoga** (408) 867-3421	Changing art exhibitions are presented in the galleries of the Villa, which is also a center for local artists, whose works are frequently shown. The arboretum includes a redwood grove, nature trails and a bird sanctuary. Many species of birds can be spotted during a single visit to this quiet, restful area.
OLD TOWN LOS GATOS University Ave. **Los Gatos**	Spanish-style shops, restaurants, art galleries and studios combine to create a pleasant experience in a shopping village different from all others. Unusual gift items, clothing, toys and a wide variety of art objects are on sale. Local artists, sculptors, potters and metalworkers display their latest creations, and visitors may watch them while they work.
BILLY JONES WILDCAT RAILROAD Oak Meadow Park University Ave. **Los Gatos** (408) 354-8320	In 1947 a retired railroad engineer, aided by friends and other enthusiasts, built this narrow-gauge steam railroad for the pleasure of the children of Santa Clara Valley. The tracks were extended in 1972 and now include a 40-foot curved wooden trestle and long grade which taxes the strength of the small engine.
LOS GATOS MUSEUM Main & Tait Sts. **Los Gatos** (408) 354-5172	This is a museum with a unique range of exhibits that are of interest to children as well as adults. Included are models of Sutter's Mill, a grist mill, the Klamath River Bridge and a 20-mule-team wagon. There is a natural history room, an antique tool collection and, most recently, the addition of historical fire-fighting equipment.

Arboretum:
Daily, 8 am to 5 pm
Art Gallery:
Daily, except Mon.
1 pm to 4 pm

Adults: 25¢ (Sat. & Sun.)
Weekdays free
Children under 12 free

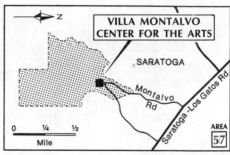

Daily, except Mon.
10 am to 9 pm
June, July & Aug.
Also Nov. 23 to Dec. 24

Free

Daily, except Mon.
during summer
11 am to 5:30 pm

Rest of year,
Sat. & Sun. only

Adults: 50¢
Children: Under 17 25¢

Daily,
Mon. through Sat.
1 pm to 4 pm

Sun. 2 pm to 4 pm

Free

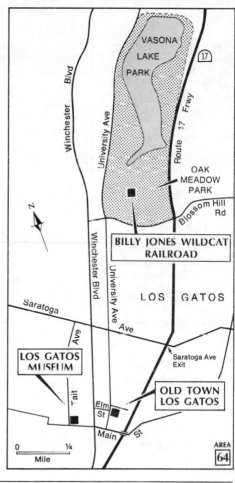

SAN JOSE BABY ZOO Kelley Park Keyes & Senter Rds. **San Jose** (408) 293-2229	This small zoo is set in beautifully landscaped grounds within Kelley Park, one of the city's most attractive park areas, which also contains the Japanese Friendship Garden, the Historical Museum, Happy Hollow, a Junior Theater, Community Center and an arboretum. The zoo has tropical birds, reptiles and animals from many parts of the world.
HAPPY HOLLOW Kelley Park Keyes & Senter Rds. **San Jose** (408) 292-8188	Within Kelley Park and close to the Zoo, this charming children's playground has a tree house, a miniature ship, a castle and many exciting things to see and do. Free puppet shows, a merry-go-round, places to climb and places to slide all combine to make the area a delightful place to visit with children.
JAPANESE FRIENDSHIP TEA GARDEN Kelley Park 1490 Senter Rd. **San Jose** (408) 294-4706	This garden was created to symbolize the ties between San Jose and its sister city of Okayama, Japan, and is patterned after the world-famous Korakuen Park. The lovely garden contains lakes, waterfalls, picturesque bridges and many flowers and shrubs. The Teahouse serves traditional Japanese luncheons, tea and cookies.
SAN JOSE HISTORICAL MUSEUM Kelley Park 635 Phelan Ave. **San Jose**	The history of the Santa Clara Valley is well depicted in the various rooms of this museum, providing visitors with an interesting glimpse into the past. There are an Indian Room, Spanish and Mexican Room, Pioneer Room and even an Old Schoolroom where typical elements of a 19th-century schoolhouse can be found.

Daily, 10 am to 4 pm

Adults: $1.00
Children: 2–14 60¢
Under 2 free.
(Combination ticket to Zoo
and Happy Hollow available)

Daily, 10 am to 4 pm

Adults: $1.00
Children: 2–14 60¢
Under 2 free
(Combination ticket to Zoo
and Happy Hollow available)

Daily, except Mon.
11 am to 5 pm

Free

Daily
Mon. through Fri.
10 am to 4:30 pm
Sat. & Sun.
12 noon to 4:30 pm

Adults: 25¢
Children 8–17 10¢
Under 8 free
Family rate: 50¢

ROSICRUCIAN PLANETARIUM & EGYPTIAN MUSEUM Park & Naglee Aves. **San Jose** (408) 295-0323	**Planetarium** Students of astronomy and lovers of nature's mysteries will enjoy these visual presentations, given in a format that can be readily understood by non-scientific minds. Vast periods of time unfold as reproduced movement of the stars and planets takes place in the domed amphitheater. The Rosicrucian Science Museum, located in the Planetarium building, houses exhibits of the physical sciences. **Egyptian Museum** A full-sized reproduction of an Egyptian tomb; rare Egyptian, Assyrian and Babylonian antiquities, and mummified bodies of high priests and animals are among the many interesting exhibits to be seen in this unusual museum.
WINCHESTER MYSTERY HOUSE State Historic Monument 525 S. Winchester Blvd. **San Jose** (408) 296-0213	The strangest dwelling in the country, this 160-room mansion was the home of Sarah L. Winchester, wife of the rifle manufacturer. After the death of her husband and infant son, a seeress told her that so long as she continued to build on to the house, she would never die. Building continued for thirty-six years—secret passages, hidden rooms (mostly with 13 windows) and doors leading nowhere. It stopped with Sarah's death at 85.
FRONTIER VILLAGE AMUSEMENT PARK 4885 Monterey Rd. **San Jose** (408) 225-1500	The wild, exciting frontier days of the 1890s are recreated in this amusement park where shoot-outs and bank robberies take place every hour on the main street. Attractions include a Ferris wheel, stagecoach, burro pack train, Indian Jim's war canoes and many others. Visitors can pan for gold, fish for trout or shop in the old general store.

20

WHEN TO GO AND WHERE TO FIND IT

Planetarium:
Daily, except Mon.
June through Sept.
1 pm to 5 pm
Oct. through May
Sat. & Sun. only
1 pm to 5 pm

Adults: $1.00
Children: Under 18 50¢

Egyptian Museum: Daily,
Sat., Sun., Mon.
12 noon to 5 pm
Tues. through Fri.
9 am to 5 pm

Free

Daily,
Summer: 9 am to 6 pm

Winter: 9 am to 4:30 pm

Adults: $3.50
Children: 5–12 $2.00
Under 5 free

Daily, mid-June to Labor Day:
Sun.–Thur. 10 am to 5 pm
Fri. & Sat. 10 am to 10 pm

Rest of year:
Sat. & Sun. 10 am to 5 pm

General admission:
Adults and children: $4.50;
(ticket includes unlimited rides plus
entertainment)

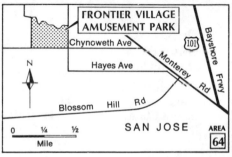

MINOLTA PLANETARIUM

De Anza College
21250 Stevens
Creek Blvd.
Cupertino

(408) 257-5552
for information on
current programs

Excellent programs are presented on a scheduled basis in this modern planetarium, which utilises a Minolta projector and 27-channel omniphonic sound system.

In a related facility at Foothill College there is also a planetarium, observatory and an electronics museum, all of which are open to the public. Telephone 948-8590, ext. 381, for complete information.

MISSION SANTA CLARA DE ASSIS

University of
Santa Clara
820 Alviso
Santa Clara

(408) 984-4242

The original mission was founded in 1777 on the banks of the Rio Guadalupe. Set amid palm and olive trees planted by the Franciscan padres, the mission was named for the founder of the famous order of nuns called the poor Clares. St. Clare of Assisi was a contemporary and spiritual daughter of St. Francis.

A disastrous flood destroyed the church on January 23, 1779, forcing a move to higher ground while a temporary mission was built. On November 19, 1781, Father Junipero Serra laid the cornerstone for a permanent adobe church.

The earthquake of 1818 severely damaged the adobe structure. Another temporary mission was established, but this too fell into disrepair during the late 1800s. The present building is a faithful reproduction, and an adjacent museum houses many artifacts from those very early days.

De SAISSET GALLERY & MUSEUM

University of
Santa Clara
Santa Clara

(408) 984-4528

The Gallery is a lively art center of the San Francisco Bay Area, located on the University campus and sharing in the great upsurge of student interest in the creative arts.

Major exhibits feature all media, including oils, water colors, sculpture and graphics. Local artists from both the campus and the surrounding community frequently hold one-man or group shows.

22

Programs:
Thurs. through Sun. 8 pm
Also at 3 pm Sat. & Sun.

Adults: $1.00
College Students 75¢
Children under 13 50¢

Daily,

Mon. through Fri.
9 am to 5 pm

Sat. 6 am to 7 pm

Sun. 6 am to 10 pm

Free

Daily, except Mon.
Tues.–Thurs. 10 am to 5 pm
Thurs. 7 pm to 9 pm
Sat. & Sun. 1 pm to 5 pm

Free

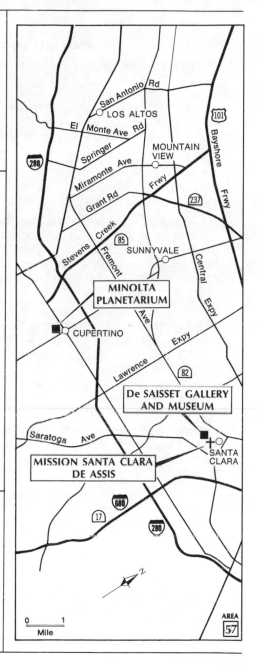

MINOLTA
PLANETARIUM

De SAISSET GALLERY
AND MUSEUM

MISSION SANTA CLARA
DE ASSIS

AREA
57

STANFORD UNIVERSITY

Guide & Visitors Services **Palo Alto**   (415) 321-2300 Ext. 2551

Stanford University is a private, coeducational residential university located on more than 8,000 acres of rolling land on the San Francisco Peninsula. The arcaded, red-tiled buildings and spacious lawns shaded by tall trees make this campus one of the most beautiful in the country.

Several tours are offered to the public, both walking and motorized. All are conducted by student guides and each tour lasts approximately one hour.

Walking Tours
For individual and very small groups the regularly scheduled walking tours leave from the Information Office at the main entrance to the campus Quadrangle. The tours culminate with a trip to the top of the Hoover Tower (there is a charge of 25¢ per person over 12 years of age for the trip).

Motorized Surrey Tour
This tour leaves from the Hoover Tower several times each day and offers a motorized trip through the campus. The maximum capacity is 6 persons each trip, on a reservation basis. The charge is 50¢ per person.

For those preferring to conduct their own tour, a "do-it-yourself" booklet, *Seeing Stanford,* is available at small cost at both the Hoover Tower and the Information Office.

Other buildings of interest which may be visited include the Leland Stanford Jr. Museum, the Stanford Art Gallery, The Hoover Institution on War, Revolution and Peace, and Stanford Memorial Church.

Stanford Linear Accelerator Center
Tours are by arrangement only. Write to the Public Information Office, Stanford Linear Accelerator Center, Stanford University, P.O. Box 4349, Stanford, Calif. 94305. (Tel: [415] 321-2300, Ext. 3469.)

Stanford University Medical Center
Tours by arrangement only. Write to Public Events, Medical School, Stanford Medical Center, Room M 121, Stanford, Calif. 94305. (Tel: [415] 321-1200, Ext. 5594)

Walking tours depart Monday through Saturday at 11 am and 2:15 pm., Sundays at 2:15 only.

Surrey Tours depart Mon. through Fri. at 10 am, 11 am, 2:15 pm and 3:15 pm.

Saturdays at 11 am, 1:15 pm, 2:15 pm and 3:15 pm. Sundays at 1:15 pm, 2:15 pm and 3:15 pm

WEST BAY MODEL RAILROAD ASSN. INC. 1090 Merrill St. **Menlo Park** (415) 322-0685	For children of all ages and train buffs who appreciate the excellence of a fine layout, this model railroad club runs three different-sized trains over 4,000 feet of track. Miniature towns, with scenery, bridges and trestles scaled to match, enhance the realism of the operation, made even more interesting by taped sound effects and a story of the history of the club.
SUNSET MAGAZINE HEADQUARTERS Willow Rd. & Middlefield Rd. **Menlo Park** (415) 321-3600	Home of the famous _Sunset_ magazine and Sunset Books, the ranch-style buildings surround some of the most beautiful gardens to be found in any business environment. Conducted tours include visits to the editorial offices, testing kitchens, advertising and conference rooms. The Western Gardens are open to visitors from 9:30 am to 4:30 pm. Mon. through Fri.
PALO ALTO JUNIOR MUSEUM & ZOO 1451 Middlefield Rd. **Palo Alto** (415) 329-2111	Arts and crafts, ceramics, two science rooms and a museum exhibit room comprise this excellent junior museum, which is part of the Nature and Science department of the city of Palo Alto. Outside, in the small zoo, enclosures house a variety of wildlife, including birds of prey, raccoons, bobcats and other creatures.
BAYLANDS NATURE INTERPRETIVE CENTER 2775 Embarcadero Rd. **Palo Alto** (415) 329-2506	The Center focuses on the conservation, ecology and natural history of the Bay Area. Pictures of local birds are on view and a plant exhibit, salt-water aquarium and various changing displays are open throughout the week. Nature movies and nature walks are given on weekends and are of particular interest to children.

3rd Fri. & 4th Wed. of
each month except Dec.
8 am to 10 pm

Free

Guided tours,
Mon. through Fri.
10:30 am, 11:30 am
1 pm, 2 pm, 3 pm

Free

Daily, except Mon.
10 am to 5 pm
Sun. 1 pm to 4 pm

Free

Daily:

Mon. through Fri.
2 pm to 5 pm

Sat. & Sun. 10 am to 5 pm

Free

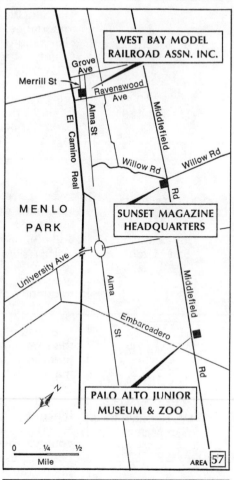

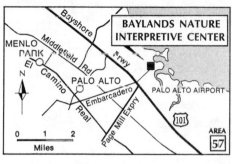

THE SANCHEZ ADOBE Linda Mar Blvd. **Pacifica** (415) 359-1881	The Sanchez Adobe is a structure of historic importance, having been the first outpost of civilization in what is now San Mateo County. Over the past 100 years the adobe has been the scene of many brilliant social gatherings, births, deaths and at least one murder. Open to the public as a small museum, the adobe contains many 19th-century furnishings and artifacts.
COYOTE POINT MUSEUM Coyote Point **San Mateo** (415) 573-2595	Live animals indigenous to the county (deer, foxes, coyotes, raccoons, squirrels, rabbits and many others) are exhibited in this small but very interesting museum. Birds, reptiles and amphibians are among the live exhibits. There are several dioramas showing the redwoods, the coast, the bayshore and the grasslands. Additional temporary exhibits are frequently on display.
SAN MATEO COUNTY HISTORICAL MUSEUM 1700 W. Hillsdale Blvd. **San Mateo** (415) 574-6441	The history of San Mateo is represented in this small museum, starting with a diorama of prehistoric times, supplemented by artifacts, mammoth teeth and other items found in the area. Additional dioramas illustrate Peninsula Indian life, Spanish and Mexican days, early American times and the great estates of the county. There are also displays of miscellaneous historical items, paintings and photographs.
MARINE WORLD —AFRICA USA Marine World Pkwy. **Redwood City** (415) 591-7676	Combining an African game collection and an oceanarium, the many exhibits include performances by trained killer whales, birds, dolphins and jungle cats. There is also a fine water-ski show that features a baby elephant and a lion. Other attractions include an underwater aquarium, puppet show and an unusual boat ride. All are covered by the admission price.

28

Wed. through Sun.
10 am to 12 noon
1 pm to 4 pm

Free

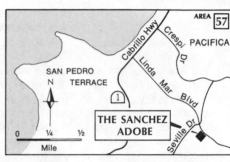

Daily,
Mon. through Sat.
9 am to 5 pm
Sun. 1 pm to 5 pm

Free

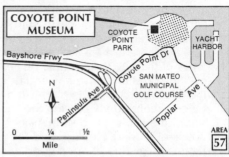

Daily, except Sun.

Mon. through Fri.
9:30 am to 4:30 pm

Sat. 10:30 am
to 4:30 pm

Free

Daily,
Memorial Day to Labor Day
9:30 am to 6:30 pm
Rest of year
Sat. & Sun. only

Adults: $5.25
Children: 5–12 $3.25
Under 5 free

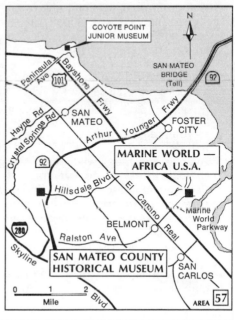

29

SAN FRANCISCO

Cosmopolitan, exciting, unlike any other city in the world, San Francisco reaches out to grasp every visitor with her extraordinary variety of moods and attractions. The city reveals its rich history on almost every street and historic buildings often stand in the shadow of ultramodern skyscrapers. Financial center of the West, San Francisco has a major industrial area and a celebrated port, but to the visitor its attractions are more cultural, romantic and subtle. Downtown San Francisco is for walkers, as much is condensed into a relatively small area. Park your car and explore the fine stores and shops. A good place to start is Union Square. Here political rallies, fashion shows and concerts are frequently held, and in summer there is a Cable Car bell-ringing contest. To explore other areas of the city, take a bus, or better still a Cable Car, and enjoy exciting rides that have few equals in other cities in the world. Visit the Financial District. Explore Chinatown, which houses the largest Oriental community outside the Far East. Climb Nob Hill, once the site of the city's grandest mansions, where two of its most famous hotels—the Mark Hopkins and the Fairmont—stand as ever-present reminders of a tradition of good and gracious living. Visit the north waterfront area, where Fishermans Wharf brings you the tang of the sea blended with appetizing smells from dozens of restaurants of all kinds and sizes. There are fine, unusual shops here; museums, art galleries and old ships to explore, and the unique Ghiradelli Square and the Cannery. Parking areas are provided. Choose a fine day and have a look at the city from the Bay. Bay cruises leave from the Fisherman's Wharf area, giving you an opportunity to sail close to infamous Alcatraz Island and the great Golden Gate and Bay bridges. When your feet ache then it is time to get in your car and follow the clearly marked 49-mile drive. Allow a half-day for this, and if you start at Civic Center near Van Ness Avenue, the blue, white and orange seagull signs will lead you through the city and eventually through beautiful Golden Gate Park. San Francisco has two fine downtown theaters where leading shows from Broadway feature some of the best performers in the country. Several small theaters and workshops located at North Beach and the north waterfront offer imaginative productions. The city has the largest permanent opera in the West, and the finest ballet, concerts and symphonies. For those who like to sample the more sophisticated areas of a city's night life, there are many bars, clubs, discotheques and eating places where entertainment of varying kinds is offered.

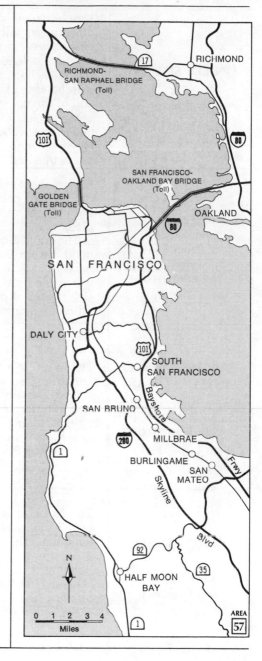

UNION SQUARE Powell, Geary Post & Stockton Sts.	Union Square is the heart of San Francisco's downtown fashionable shopping district. Fine stores selling men's and women's clothing, art galleries, bookstores, jewelers and specialty shops offer a wide variety of quality merchandise. Street vendors and musicians add to the colorful scene. Many civic events are held in the Square: flower festivals, musical shows, political meetings, and at Christmas time there is much tree and shrub decoration.
A WORLD OF OIL Standard Oil of California 555 Market St. **San Francisco** (415) 894-4895	A permanent exhibit that tells the story of the oil industry, past and present, through working models, moving displays and a motion picture. The short film illustrates how oil is developed within the earth over a tremendous passage of time and shows its discovery and use in the past. Another feature is three life-size historical dioramas. A variety of actual oil-field equipment can also be seen.
SAN FRANCISCO MUSEUM OF ART 4th Flr., Veterans Bldg. Van Ness & McAllister **San Francisco** (415) 863-8800	This is a fine art gallery specializing in contemporary work from throughout the world. The constantly changing exhibits range from painting and photography to sculpture, design, graphic art and architecture. The many artists living in San Francisco and the surrounding Bay area are well represented.
CIVIC CENTER Van Ness Ave. & McAllister St. **San Francisco**	San Francisco's Civic Center covers more than 7 square blocks and contains many fine buildings. The lofty dome of the City Hall dominates the area, which includes the State Building, Public Library, Civic Auditorium, Federal Office Building, Veterans Memorial Building and the Opera House. Beneath the spacious Civic Center Plaza is Brooks Hall, a vast underground exhibit area.

Daily,
except Sat. & Sun.
9 am to 4 pm

Free

Daily, except Mon.

Tues. through Fri.
10 am to 10 pm

Sat. & Sun.
10 am to 5 pm

Free (except for
special exhibitions)

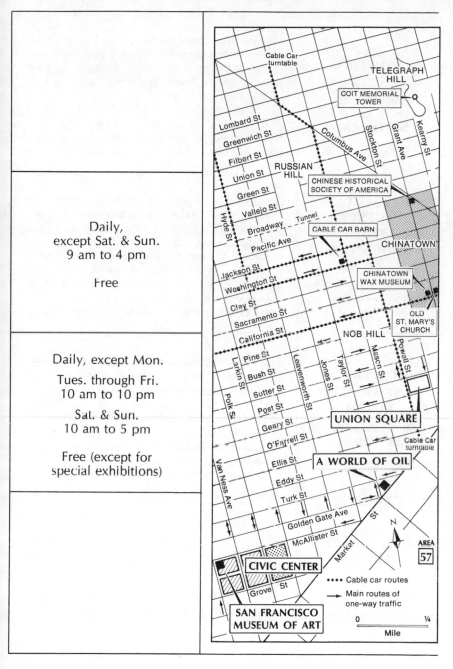

NOB HILL California, Sacramento, Jones & Taylor Sts. **San Francisco**	Elegant apartment buildings and hotels now occupy this famed hilltop area, once the home of the men who built fortunes in gold mining and railroading during the latter half of the 19th century. The gothic Grace Cathedral is also on Nob Hill. One of the oldest cathedrals in the country, it was established in 1863. Free guided tours are given daily, Mon. through Fri.
MUSEUM OF MONEY OF THE AMERICAN WEST Bank of California 400 California St. **San Francisco** (415) 765-2593	The museum is located on the lower level of the main hall of the Bank and contains many examples of currency as it pertained to the roaring days of the Old West. Before the establishment of the U.S. Mint in San Francisco, privately minted coins and gold nuggets were used for money. Many of these are on display, together with shiny counterfeit coins and banking memorabilia.
WELLS FARGO BANK HISTORY ROOM 420 Montgomery St. **San Francisco** (415) 396-2648	The history of Wells Fargo and the Old West will be found in this museum where relics of gold rush days—nuggets, treasure boxes, old money, miners' picks and shovels and other tools—date from 1848 to the fire and earthquake of 1906. A large collection of stamps and postmarks is on display; also a well-preserved Concord stagecoach once used to carry the mail.
OLD ST. MARY'S CHURCH 660 California St. **San Francisco** (415) 986-4388	This fine old church was dedicated in 1854, and for half a century it was the cathedral seat of the Roman Catholic Diocese of the Pacific Coast. The structure is patterned after a church in Spain. In 1906 the interior was destroyed by fire. It was rebuilt, and at a later date a wing was added to house the Paulist library.

Mon. through Thur.
10 am to 3:30 pm

Fri. 10 am to 5 pm

Free

Every banking day,
10 am to 3 pm

Free

Daily,
6:30 am to 7 pm

Free

•••• Cable car routes

→ Main routes of
one-way traffic

N

0   ¼
Mile

THE EMBARCADERO

COIT MEMORIAL
TOWER

TELEGRAPH
HILL

Columbus Ave

Stockton St

Grant Ave

Kearny St

Montgomery

Sansome St

Mason St

Powell St

CHINESE HISTORICAL
SOCIETY OF AMERICA

St

Battery St

OLD ST. MARY'S
CHURCH

WELLS FARGO BANK
HISTORY ROOM

PACIFIC COAST
STOCK EXCHANGE

CHINATOWN

CABLE CAR BARN

Sacramento St

California St

CHINATOWN
WAX MUSEUM

Pine St

NOB HILL

MUSEUM OF MONEY

Bush St

Sutter St

Post St

UNION SQUARE

Geary St

CHINESE HISTORICAL SOCIETY OF AMERICA 17 Adler Place (off 1140 Grant Ave.) **San Francisco** (415) 391-1188	Chinese influence in the development of California and San Francisco is well represented in this small museum. Many exhibits have been contributed by Chinese societies and include historical papers, photographs and artifacts pertaining to the days of gold-mining and railroad construction. There are also Buddhist leaflets, ceremonial swords and clothing.
CHINATOWN Broadway, Bush, Kearney & Stockton Sts. **San Francisco**	San Francisco's Chinatown is the largest Oriental community outside of the Orient—a 16-block area packed with fascinating shops, stores, restaurants and markets, complete with the many exotic sounds and smells of the Far East. See Chinatown on foot; stroll leisurely along Grant Avenue, where curio shops and import stores abound, and explore the missions, temples, schools and theaters.
CHINATOWN WAX MUSEUM 601 Grant Ave. **San Francisco** (415) 392-1011	This unusual folk and art museum depicts scenes from the early days of Chinatown as well as highlights of 4,000 years of Chinese history. There are 33 lifelike tableaux with 115 wax figures, crafted by skilled artisans in Hong Kong. The scenes range from a bustling fortune cookie factory to the magnificent opulence of the most imperial court of Kublai Khan.
PACIFIC STOCK EXCHANGE, INC. 301 Pine St. **San Francisco** (415) 392-6533	The Pacific Stock Exchange handles more stock transactions than any other exchange outside of New York City. Visitors are welcome to watch operations on the trading floor from a glass-enclosed balcony. The operation would not be of interest to very young children; for adults some prior knowledge of the securities business would be advantageous.

Daily, except Mon.
1 pm to 5 pm

Free

Daily,
10 am to 11 pm.

Adults: $1.50
Children: 6–12 $1.00
Under 6 free

Daily,
except Sat. & Sun.
8:30 am to 12 noon

Free
(Telephone for a
reservation preferably
two weeks in advance)

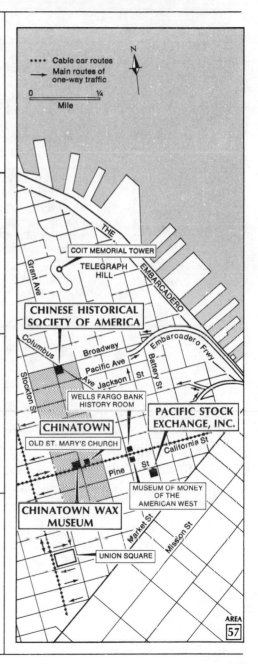

CALIFORNIA DIVISION OF MINES & GEOLOGY Mineral Exhibit & Library Rm. 2022, Ferry Bldg. **San Francisco** (415) 557-0633 (museum) 557-0308 (library)	Thousands of mineral, rock and ore specimens are on display in this well-organized museum. The Dana System exhibit of minerals is one of the largest and most beautiful in California. Replicas of famous gold nuggets, including the beautiful "Fricot" from El Dorado County, can be seen by visitors. Bay Area gem and mineral societies maintain displays in the museum on a rotating basis.
COIT MEMORIAL TOWER Telegraph Hill **San Francisco**	One of the city's best views can be had from Coit Tower, a 210-foot-high monument to San Francisco's volunteer firemen. The structure is named after Lillie Coit, a celebrated wealthy eccentric whose varied and unusual interests included riding with the fire companies. The tower is a landmark at the top of Telegraph Hill, an area that was once an artist's colony and is now a fashionable residential district.
CABLE CAR BARN 1201 Mason St. **San Francisco.** (415) 558-3382	At a time when buses and airplanes are taking an ever-increasing share of public transportation, it is refreshing to find one old, unique method of travel still in operation, retained by affectionate public demand against the cries of those who favor more progressive forms of movement. The first cable car made its trial run in 1873, and at its peak of popularity more than a dozen lines traversed the city. Duplicate systems were in operation in many major American cities, but today most of these have disappeared and only three lines still operate in San Francisco. The Cable Car Barn houses the huge wheels and cables that operate the system. Visitors can watch the operation from a platform, see a photographic history of the city's cable cars, Victorian memorabilia and the first cable car, constructed in San Francisco a hundred years ago.

Mon. through Fri.
8 am to 5 pm
1st Sat. of the month,
10 am to 12 noon

Free

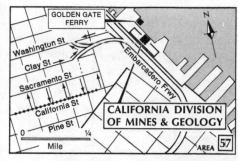

Daily,
Mon.–Fri. 11 am to 4:15 pm
Sat. & Sun. 10 am to 4:30 pm

Adults: 25¢
Children: under 12 free
(Elevator service
to top of tower)

Daily,
Mon. through Thurs.
10 am to 6 pm
Fri. Sat. & Sun.
10 am to 10 pm

Free

39

ALCATRAZ ISLAND Harbor Carriers, Inc. Pier 43, Fisherman's Wharf **San Francisco** (415) 398-1141	For many years Alcatraz Island was a stern federal prison, known as "The Rock." The island is now open to the public through guided tours conducted by Harbor Carriers, Inc. Boats leave pier 43 at regular intervals. Reservations are essential. The tour involves some strenuous walking. Dress warmly, particularly in poor weather, and take a sweater with you at all times.
TIBURON & ANGEL ISLAND FERRIES Harbor Tours, Inc. Pier 43½ Fisherman's Wharf (415) 398-1141	Angel Island State Park is a federal and state refuge for wildlife and plants and a tranquil and delightful place to visit. It is reached by a short trip on one of the red-and-white boats of Harbor Carriers. Visitors can enjoy Elephant Train tours in open-air coaches, hiking, bicycling, fishing from the pier and sunbathing. Swimming is not permitted. Admission to the State Park: Adults 25¢ Children under 12, free.
SAN FRANCISCO BAY CRUISE Harbor Tours, Inc. Pier 43½ Fisherman's Wharf **San Francisco** (415) 398-1141	Specially designed sightseeing ships, each carrying up to 500 passengers, make regular cruises around San Francisco Bay. The boats pass under both the Golden Gate Bridge and the San Francisco-Oakland Bay Bridge, sailing close enough to Alcatraz Island to give passengers a close-up view of the former prison. The 75-minute tours are guided with brief descriptions of the many places of interest to be seen.
GOLDEN GATE FERRY Ferry Building Embarcadero **San Francisco** (415) 892-8833	The Golden Gate Ferry plies sturdily across the bay between the San Francisco Ferry Building and Sausalito, passing the island of Alcatraz. Approximately a 45-minute journey. Light refreshments may be purchased on board, and this short trip, especially in good weather, can be a most enjoyable experience and great fun for children. The ferry leaves Pier 1 at regular intervals, about 90 minutes apart.

Daily service
(Telephone for
current schedule)

Adults: $2.00
Children: 5–12 $1.00
Under 5 free

Daily,
Jun. 1–Sept. 10
Limited service rest of year

Round-trip rates:

San Francisco or Berkeley
to Angel Island, Adults: $3.00
Children: 5–11 $2.00

Berkeley to Tiburon
Adults: $2.75
Children 5–11 $1.40

Daily, first cruise 10 am
then at 30–45 min. intervals
(Telephone for current schedule)

Adults: $3.50
Children: 12–17 $2.50
5–11 $1.50
Under 5 free

One-way fare: Adults: 75¢
Children: 6–12 25¢
Under 6 free

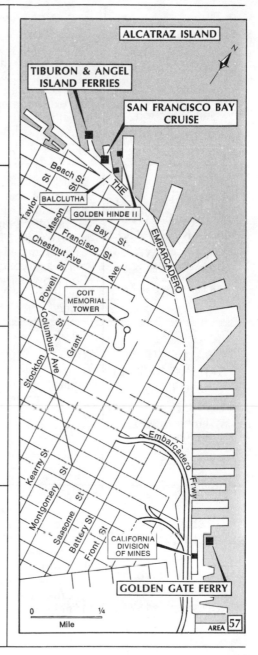

ALCATRAZ ISLAND

TIBURON & ANGEL
ISLAND FERRIES

SAN FRANCISCO BAY
CRUISE

Beach St

Taylor St

BALCLUTHA

GOLDEN HINDE II

Mason St

Francisco St

Bay St

Chestnut Ave

Powell St

COIT
MEMORIAL
TOWER

Columbus Ave

Grant St

Stockton St

THE EMBARCADERO

Embarcadero

Kearny St

Montgomery St

Sansome St

Battery St

Front St

CALIFORNIA
DIVISION
OF MINES

Embarcadero Frwy

GOLDEN GATE FERRY

0   ¼
Mile

AREA 57

41

RIPLEY'S BELIEVE IT OR NOT MUSEUM 175 Jefferson St. Fisherman's Wharf **San Francisco** (415) 673-9765	Over 2,000 oddities created by the mind and hand of man are on display in this extraordinary museum. Many of them were personally collected by the famed cartoonist, Robert Leroy Ripley. Among the strange and almost unbelievable exhibits are such wonders as the world's smallest violin, which actually plays; a replica of Lincoln's log cabin made from 16,360 pennies, and a double-eyed man.
THE ENCHANTED WORLD OF OLD SAN FRANCISCO Fisherman's Wharf **San Francisco** (415) 441-6262	Board an 1880 cable car for a fascinating adventure tour of Old San Francisco. This panoramic history of the city, from the days of the '49ers right up to the present, is presented with 150 gaily costumed, electronically animated characters. Tableaux include a New Year's festival in Chinatown, The Great Earthquake and Fire, the Panama-Pacific Exhibition and many others.
BALCLUTHA SAILING VESSEL MUSEUM Pier 43 Embarcadero **San Francisco** (415) 982-1886	The Balclutha is one of the last surviving square-rigged sailing vessels and is now a floating museum. The fittings, clothing and other mementos provide a glimpse of life aboard ship in the days when these great vessels sailed around Cape Horn and came to San Francisco during the days of the gold rush and Barbary Coast.
GOLDEN HINDE II Pier 41, Fisherman's Wharf, **San Francisco** (415) 392-6552	This is a full-size replica of the famous vessel in which Sir Francis Drake circumnavigated the world between 1557 and 1580. The sturdy square-rigged galleon was built in England and sailed 10,381 miles to its present berth in San Francisco. Cross the gangplank and step into the 16th-century warship, fully armed for battle and adventure on the high seas!

Daily,
June to Sept.
9 am to 11 pm,
Oct. to May
10 am to 10 pm

Adults: $2.50
Children: 12 and under $1.25

Daily, May through Aug.
9 am to midnight;
Sept. through April,
Sun. through Thurs.
10 am to 10 pm
Fri. & Sat.
10 am to midnight.

Adults: $1.00
Children: 6–13 50¢

Daily,
9 am to 11 pm

Adults: $2.00
Children: 12–17 $1.00
6–11 25¢
Under 6 free

Daily,
10 am to 6 pm

Adults: $2.00
Senior Citizens: $1.50
Children 13–17 $1.50
4–12 $1.00
Under 4 free

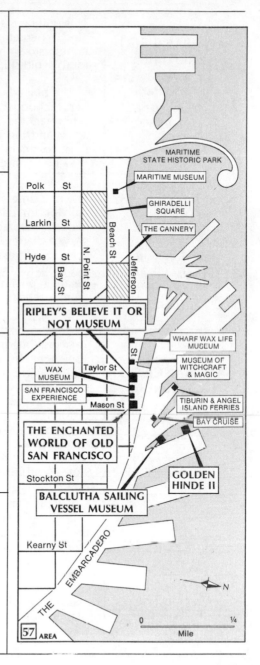

MARITIME
STATE HISTORIC PARK
MARITIME MUSEUM
Polk   St
GHIRADELLI
SQUARE
Larkin   St
Beach St
THE CANNERY
Hyde   St
N. Point St
Jefferson
Bay St
RIPLEY'S BELIEVE IT OR NOT MUSEUM
WHARF WAX LIFE MUSEUM
St
MUSEUM OF WITCHCRAFT & MAGIC
WAX MUSEUM   Taylor St
SAN FRANCISCO EXPERIENCE
TIBURIN & ANGEL ISLAND FERRIES
Mason St
BAY CRUISE
THE ENCHANTED WORLD OF OLD SAN FRANCISCO
GOLDEN HINDE II
Stockton St
BALCLUTHA SAILING VESSEL MUSEUM
Kearny St
EMBARCADERO
THE
57 AREA
0   ¼
Mile
N

SAN FRANCISCO MARITIME State **Historic Park** 2905 Hyde St. **San Francisco** (415) 441-2116	This unique State Historic Park has been created to perpetuate California'a vigorous maritime history and provide a permanent home for four old ships—a living monument to the past. The black-hulled *C. A. Thayer* was a lumber schooner, the *Wapama* a steam schooner, the *Alma* a shallow draft sailing scow and the *Eureka* the last paddle-wheel ferry to operate in San Francisco Bay. All may be boarded.
SAN FRANCISCO MARITIME MUSEUM Musem Building Foot of Polk St. **San Francisco** (415) 776-1175	The maritime history of San Francisco is visually portrayed here with an outstanding collection of artifacts, harpoons, anchors, scrimshaw, diaries, ships' logs and full-scale portions of vessels. Many fine models, accurate to the smallest detail, replicate sail and steamships, among them lumber schooners, grain ships, barkentines and navy vessels.
SAN FRANCISCO EXPERIENCE Fisherman's Wharf Jefferson St. **San Francisco** (415) 474-7272	This multimedia production is presented to audiences in a small, specially designed theater. Thirty computerized projectors, stereo sound and a giant 180-degree screen vividly recreate 200 years of Bay area history. The romantic days of the gold rush, the terrifying 1906 earthquake and fire, foghorns, the sound of the ocean, night clubs, shows and other scenic delights go into the program.
FISHERMAN'S WHARF Jones & Jefferson Sts. **San Francisco**	Fine Italian and seafood restaurants, markets, stores, souvenir shops and import houses line the waterfront, where fishing boats unload their catch. Harbor cruises and helicopter rides are available. Picturesque sights, pungent smells, kettles of steaming crabs, seafood cocktails and sour-dough bread are part of the open-air fish market scene on Jefferson St. From downtown, take the cable car to its Taylor and Bay Sts. turntable.

44

WHEN TO GO AND WHERE TO FIND IT

Daily,
June to Oct.
10 am to 6:30 pm
Nov. to May
10 am to 5 pm

Adults: 75¢
Children: 6–17 25¢
Under 6 free

Daily,
10 am to 5 pm

Adults: $1.00
Children: 7–17 50¢
Under 7 free

Daily,
11:15 am to 9 pm
Fri. & Sat. to 11:15 pm
(Shows every 45 minutes)

Adults: $2.00
Children: 6–11 $1.00
Under 6 free

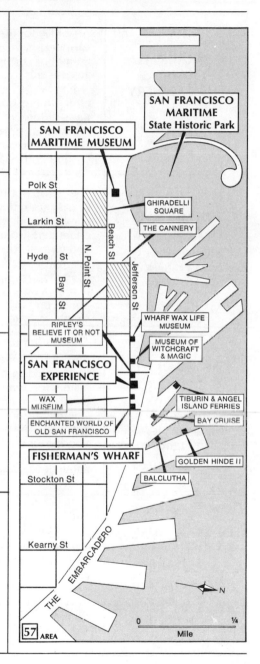

SAN FRANCISCO
MARITIME
State Historic Park

SAN FRANCISCO
MARITIME MUSEUM

Polk St

GHIRADELLI
SQUARE

Larkin St

THE CANNERY

Beach St

Hyde   St

N. Point St

Jefferson St

Bay

St

WHARF WAX LIFE
MUSEUM

RIPLEY'S
BELIEVE IT OR NOT
MUSEUM

MUSEUM OF
WITCHCRAFT
& MAGIC

SAN FRANCISCO
EXPERIENCE

WAX
MUSEUM

TIBURIN & ANGEL
ISLAND FERRIES

BAY CRUISE

ENCHANTED WORLD OF
OLD SAN FRANCISCO

FISHERMAN'S WHARF

GOLDEN HINDE II

Stockton St

BALCLUTHA

Kearny St

THE EMBARCADERO

N

0   ¼

Mile

57 AREA

GHIRARDELLI SQUARE & THE CANNERY Near Fisherman's Wharf **San Francisco**	An old chocolate factory and a disused fish cannery have been transformed into two delightful shopping areas, with open-air plazas, restaurants and strolling musicians. Numerous small shops and art galleries offer interesting merchandise from many parts of the world, ranging from costly clothing and art objects to inexpensive souvenirs. No visitor to San Francisco should miss these unique and charming attractions.
WHARF WAX LIFE MUSEUM 295 Jefferson St. **San Francisco** (415) 776-6437	The worlds of religion, history, literature and fantasy are depicted in a large variety of displays and exhibits which include many characters from children's fairytales. Hansel and Gretel, Rip Van Winkel and other favorites will delight young visitors. For the more adventuresome, some of the names from horror fiction are on hand to chill you, including Dracula and Frankenstein's monster.
MUSEUM OF WITCHCRAFT & MAGIC 235 Jefferson St. Fisherman's Wharf **San Francisco** (415) 673-9765	The strange, weird world of the supernatural is depicted in this museum, which traces the history of man and his superstitions down through the ages. Alchemists, wizards, warlocks and witches, together with ancestor worship, voodoo, the animal magic of primitive man and the magic of today are represented in displays incorporating lifelike wax figures.
THE WAX MUSEUM AT FISHERMAN'S WHARF 145 Jefferson St. **San Francisco** (415) 885-4834	Two hundred life-size wax figures, specially created by Josephine Tussaud of London, are dramatically displayed in 60 scenes. There is a tribute to the World's great religions and a Hall of Famous people. Beautifully costumed figures populate Fairyland in Wax and, for the brave, The Chamber of Horrors recreates scenes of murder and torture.

WHEN TO GO AND WHERE TO FIND IT

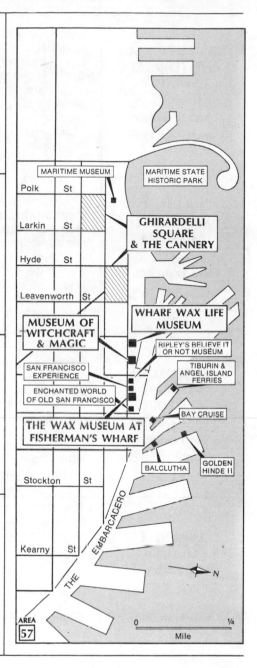

Daily, 9:30 am to 10:30 pm

Adults: $1.50
Children 6–12 75¢
Under 6 free

Daily, 10 am to 10 pm
Adults: $2.50
Children: 6–12 $1.25
Under 6 free

Daily, May through Aug.
9 am to midnight

Sept. through April

Sun.–Thurs. 10 am to 10 pm
Fri. & Sat. 10 am to midnight

Adults: $2.00
Children: 6–12 $1.00
Under 6 free

MARITIME MUSEUM

Polk   St

MARITIME STATE
HISTORIC PARK

Larkin   St

GHIRARDELLI
SQUARE
& THE CANNERY

Hyde   St

Leavenworth   St

WHARF WAX LIFE
MUSEUM

MUSEUM OF
WITCHCRAFT
& MAGIC

RIPLEY'S BELIEVE IT
OR NOT MUSEUM

SAN FRANCISCO
EXPERIENCE

TIBURIN &
ANGEL ISLAND
FERRIES

ENCHANTED WORLD
OF OLD SAN FRANCISCO

BAY CRUISE

THE WAX MUSEUM AT
FISHERMAN'S WHARF

Stockton   St

BALCLUTHA

GOLDEN
HINDE II

THE EMBARCADERO

Kearny   St

N

AREA
57

0   ¼
Mile

CALIFORNIA HISTORICAL SOCIETY 2090 Jackson St. **San Francisco** (415) 567-1848	The Society maintains two buildings in the city that are open to the public. The Mansion, noted for its beautiful floors and woodwork, is the headquarters, at 2090 Jackson St., where elegant furnishings, paintings and prints by California artists of an earlier era are on display. Schubert Hall, 2099 Pacific Ave., houses the library and the largest genealogical collection in the state.
PIONEER MEMORIAL MUSEUM 655 Presidio Ave. **San Francisco** (415) 861-8000 Ext. 210	Relics, photographs and fire-fighting equipment fill this small museum, depicting more than 100 years of San Francisco Fire Department history. The old wagons, engines, chief's buggy, an ornate hand pumper (vintage 1849), fire horns, hoses, helmets and other items make an interesting comparison with the highly efficient, modern equipment of today.
MUSEUM OF RUSSIAN CULTURE 2450 Sutter St. **San Francisco** (415) 921-7631	Memoirs, paintings, manuscripts, newspapers, photographs and other artifacts of prerevolutionary days in Russia have been gathered from throughout the world and assembled in this small museum. Personal items from the families of the Czars, including photographs and medals, letters from Tolstoy and others and paintings by Russian artists are on display.
JAPANESE CULTURAL TRADE CENTER Post, Geary, Laguna & Fillmore Sts. **San Francisco**	The Japanese Consulate, a 14-story hotel, restaurants, a variety of trade shops, showrooms and other commercial ventures are part of this complex of handsome white buildings, done in a modern oriental style. Flower arranging, Japanese painting and ceramics are frequently demonstrated in the arcade. The spacious Peace Plaza contains a 5-tiered Peace Pagoda standing in the center of a reflecting pool; at night a gracious landmark.

48

Daily,
except Sun. and Mon.

Tues. through Fri.
10 am to 4 pm

Sat. 1 pm to 4 pm.

Free

Daily, 1 pm to 5 pm

Free

Sat. only,
11 am to 3 pm

Free

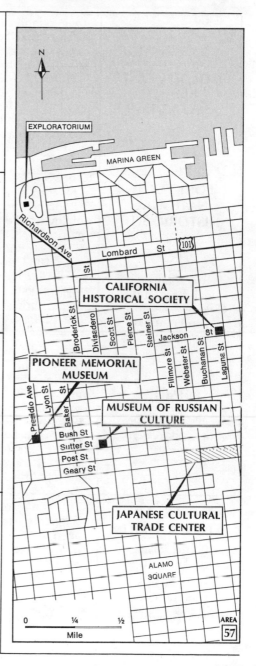

GOLDEN GATE BRIDGE San Francisco	One of the longest single-span suspension bridges ever built, this famous bridge dominates the bay, linking San Francisco with Marin County and the Redwood HIghway (US 101). Magnificent views of the San Francisco skyline can be seen if you walk out to the middle of the bridge. Cars may be parked at the toll plaza and for a nominal 10¢ fee you can enjoy views denied the automobile traveler.
FORT POINT NATIONAL HISTORIC SITE In the Presidio under the southern anchorage of the Golden Gate Bridge **San Francisco**	This unusual structure was built between 1853 and 1861 to guard against the entrance of any hostile fleet into San Francisco Bay. A garrison of 150 soldiers manned the fort, which was armed with 127 huge cannon. In 1887 the fort was inactivated. It is of particular interest to history buffs and photographers and an excellent example of the coastal brick forts built by army engineers in the 1800s.
PRESIDIO **San Francisco** (415) 561-3870	One of the oldest military reservations in the nation, the splendidly scenic Presidio is headquarters for the U.S. Sixth Army. Comprising 1,500 acres of wooded and hilly terrain, the reservation fronts on the Golden Gate, and is laced with winding roads. A hiking trail covering 7 miles is open to the public, beginning at the Lombard St. gate. Guided tours for groups can be arranged through the Tour Director.
EXPLORATORIUM (In the Palace of Fine Arts) 3601 Lyon St. **San Francisco** (415) 563-7337	This is a splended new kind of participatory science museum where visitors, are encouraged to touch, see, hear and explore the many intriguing exhibits. Objects range from rocket ships to ocean wave simulators. High school student "explainers" are on hand to assist in the use of equipment that challenges our command of sight and sound, teaching how we all rely on our senses to decipher the world around us.

Southbound
passenger-car toll 50¢

northbound free

Daily,
10 am to 5 pm

Free

Daily

Free (For guided tours,
write Tour Director,
Sixth U.S. Army,
Presidio of
San Francisco, 94129)

Wed. through Sun.
1 pm to 5 pm

Wed. evening,
7 pm to 9:30 pm

Donation

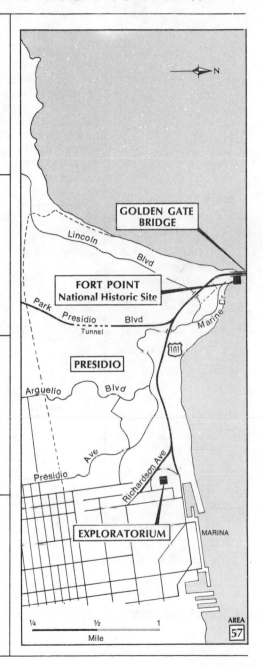

AREA
57

51

SAN FRANCISCO ZOOLOGICAL GARDENS

Zoo Rd. at
Skyline Blvd.
San Francisco

(415) 558-4461

An excellent collection of animals, birds and reptiles from all parts of the world is housed in surroundings similar to their natural habitat. Of particular interest are some of the rarer creatures that cannot be seen in many zoos, including the okapi, snow leopard, musk ox, white rhinocerous and the pigmy hippopotamus.

The zoo has plenty of free parking, a merry-go-round, miniature steam railroad and a 20-minute guided tour aboard an elephant train.

STORYLAND CHILDREN'S ZOO
(Entrance near the merry-go-round)

Boys and girls have a chance to feed and pet dozens of animals, both wild and domestic, and also watch a Penguin Show. Children can have fun in the land of nursery rhymes where real animals—some portraying Peter Rabbit, the Three Little Pigs and Mary's Little Lamb—are waiting for their small visitors. Parents should note that the zoo is close to the ocean and the air can be quite cool at times.

CALIFORNIA PALACE OF THE LEGION OF HONOR

Lincoln Park
San Francisco

(415) 558-2881

This graceful building was presented to the city in 1924 by Mr. & Mrs. Adolph B. Spreckels as a museum of painting and sculpture dedicated to the memory of California soldiers who fell in the First World War.

The collections are predominantly French, in keeping with the intent of the building's donors, and among the highlights is a splended Louis XVI salon. Rodin's great sculpture, "Thinker," stands outside the museum.

Daily, 10 am to 5 pm
Closes at 5 pm
in winter months

Adults: 50¢
Children under 16 free

Admission to the
Children's Zoo is
25¢ for adults;
children ages 1–13,
15¢; under 2 free.

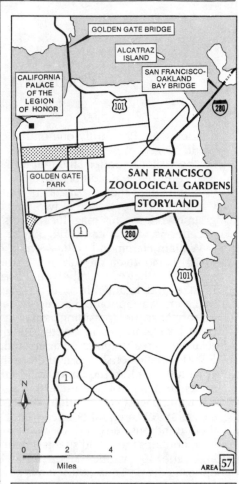

Daily,
10 am to 5 pm

Free

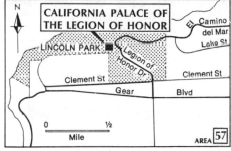

GOLDEN GATE PARK

San Francisco

Golden Gate Park, truly one of the great metropolitan parks of the world, covers more than 1,000 acres of lush grassland. It is difficult for the visitor to understand that in the early days of San Francisco, this same rea was comprised of nothing but shifting sand dunes. Fortunately for the inhabitants of the city and its many visitors, the vision and perseverence of two men during the late 1800s laid the groundwork for this magnificent park, so that today, with very few exceptions, visitors can walk, play or picnic anywhere on the grass.

William Hammond Hall was appointed first park superintendent in 1871 and given the job of transforming the barren sands into a green area that eventually would surpass New York's Central Park in size and beauty. In 1887 a Scots landscape gardener, John McLaren, was appointed as his successor and for the next 56 years he served as the "presiding genius of Golden Gate Park." McLaren drilled wells to provide water, fought politicians and city hall to retain the area's natural contours and eventually planted more than 5,000 varieties of shrubs and more than a million trees.

To fully explore the park would take several leisurely days. The principal places of interest within its confines are detailed on the following pages. But, in addition, the visitor should endeavor to see the John McLaren Rhododendron Dell, where 20 acres of rare rhododendrons surround a statue to the famed gardener. The park itself contains the world's largest collection of these shrubs, exhibiting some 300 varieties. For music lovers, the Music Concourse opposite the de Young Museum is a setting for concerts given by the Municipal Band, usually on fair-weather Sundays and holidays, between 2 and 4:30 pm.

Boating enthusiasts will enjoy Stowe Lake, the largest of the park's many artificial lakes and central reservoir for the park's irrigation system. Rowboats and motorboats may be rented, and there is a snackbar close to the dock. Tree-lined walks border the lake in the center of which is Strawberry Hill, a wooded island that may be reached by connecting bridges. A stiff 5-minute walk to the summit provides some good views on a clear day. Close by, Huntington Falls is a refreshing sight as it cascades in a 75-foot drop. The falls were a gift from railroad magnate Collis P. Huntington and, of course, were planned and arranged by the indefatigable McLaren.

In the wooded meadow to the north of Main Drive the famous herd of buffalo can be seen, peacefully grazing. The fences of the buffalo paddock have been carefully disguised by landscaping so that the animals appear to be roaming at large. Deer, elk, antelope and sheep also enjoy the tranquility of the park, along with thousands of visitors.

JAPANESE TEA GARDEN Golden Gate Park **San Francisco** (415) 752-1131	Adjacent to the de Young Museum, this delightful oriental garden area has waterfalls, bridges, bamboo-fenced walks, a sparkling pool and 5-roofed pagodas. The garden is especially attractive when the cherry blossom is in flower in the spring. Tea and cookies are served in the Japanese Tea House every day from 10:30 am to 5:30 pm
THE STRYBING ARBORETUM South Drive Golden Gate Park (415) 661-0822	More than five thousand varieties and species of shrubs and plants from all over the world, carefully arranged and labelled according to geographic origin, will be found growing in this 60-acre area. Visitors will find the demonstration gardens of particular interest, as they provide ideas for plant selection, planting design and landscape construction.
M. H. de YOUNG MUSEUM Golden Gate Park **San Francisco** (415) 558-2887	This very fine museum was opened in 1895, following a campaign instigated by Michael de Young, publisher of the San Francisco Chronicle, who proposed that the profits of the California International Exposition of 1894 be used to create and house a permanent collection of art. In 1926 the original buildings were torn down and replaced with two wings, extending from either side of a central tower. In 1966 a special wing was added to house the Avery Brundage collection of oriental art. Visitors may view over 6,000 treasures spanning 60 centuries of Asian civilization. The museum houses outstanding and varied art collections, including works by famous American and European artists, sculpture, tapestries, stained-glass windows, furniture and decorative arts.

Daily,
8 am to dusk

Free

Daily,

Mon. through Fri.
8 am to 4:30 pm

Sat. & Sun.
10 am to 5 pm

Free

Daily,
10 am to 5 pm
Free

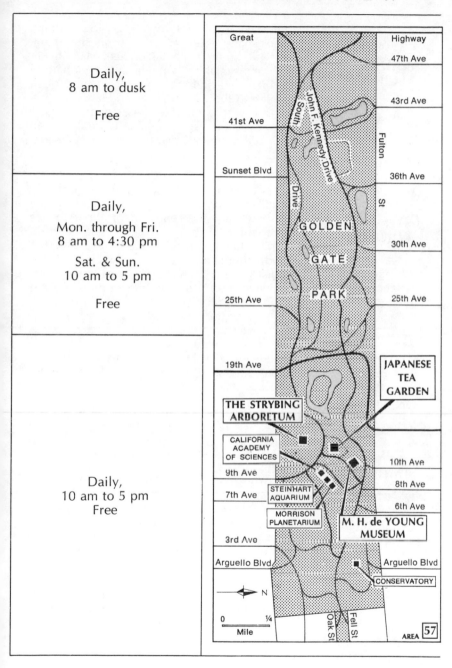

Great ... Highway

47th Ave

43rd Ave

41st Ave

Sunset Blvd

36th Ave

John F. Kennedy Drive

South Drive

Fulton St

GOLDEN

30th Ave

GATE

25th Ave ... 25th Ave

PARK

19th Ave

JAPANESE TEA GARDEN

THE STRYBING ARBORETUM

CALIFORNIA ACADEMY OF SCIENCES

10th Ave

9th Ave

8th Ave

STEINHART AQUARIUM

7th Ave

6th Ave

MORRISON PLANETARIUM

M. H. de YOUNG MUSEUM

3rd Ave

Arguello Blvd. ... Arguello Blvd

CONSERVATORY

N

0 ... ¼
Mile

Oak St

Fell St

AREA 57

CALIFORNIA ACADEMY OF SCIENCES Golden Gate Park **San Francisco** (415) 221-5100	Displays of minerals, fossils, geology, botany and space science are among the many exhibits in the Halls of Science. Magnificent dioramas of animals and birds in their natural habitat will be found in the Simson African Hall and the North American Hall. In the adjoining Steinhart Aquarium more than 10,000 fish, amphibians, reptiles and aquatic mammals can be seen in 197 separate tanks.
THE STEINHART AQUARIUM California Academy of Sciences Bldg. Golden Gate Park	This is an excellent aquarium not only for adults but for young children, as many of the displays are low enough for them to see everything easily. The tanks contain a great variety of fish and other marine creatures, including seahorses, eels, starfish, dolphins and exotic shellfish. An artificial tide pool is a most popular attraction in this splendid exhibition of marine life.
THE CONSERVATORY North of Main Dr. Golden Gate Park	Modeled after the conservatory at Kew Gardens, England, the wood and glass structure houses tropical plants and flowers from many parts of the world. Lush foliage, brightly colored crotons from the East Indies, orchids, hibiscus, ferns and rare cycads grow in profusion in a warm and humid atmosphere that duplicates the tropical climates of their native lands.
MORRISON PLANETARIUM California Academy of Sciences Golden Gate Park **San Francisco** (415) 752-8268	A circular theater seating 450 persons enables visitors to watch spectacular celestial displays that encompass such subjects as comets, cosmic evolution and a very popular annual show, "The Christmas Star." Show times and programs are subject to change without notice. Children under 5 admitted by special permission only.

58

Daily, 10 am to 5 pm
In summer:
10 am to 9 pm

Adults: 50¢
Children: 12–17 25¢
Under 12 free

Admission included
in entrance
to Science Bldg.
(see above)

Daily,
8 am to 4:50 pm

Free

Daily,
Show times vary
Extra shows
Sat. Sun & holidays.
(Telephone for
information and programs)

Adults: $1.50
Children 6–17 50¢
Under 6 free

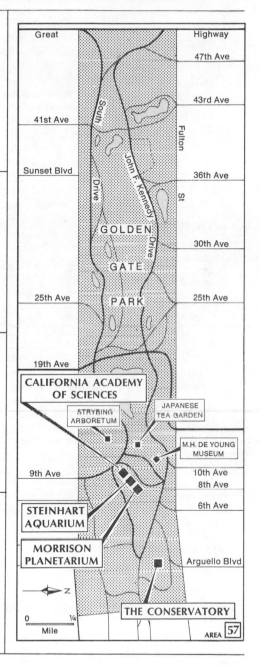

SAN FRANCISCO-OAKLAND BAY BRIDGE San Francisco	The world's longest steel bridge was completed in 1936 at a cost of $79,500,000 and is a combination of cantilevered and suspension sections divided by an island with a connecting tunnel. With a total reach of 8¼ miles, the twin-level structure carries eastbound traffic on the lower deck and westbound traffic on the deck above. The bridge provides direct communication between San Francisco and the East Bay cities.
OAKLAND MUSEUM 1000 Oak St. **Oakland** (415) 273-3401	A 3-level complex of galleries and gardens encompasses California history, art and ecology, with additional changing exhibitions. The history level covers a span from 3000 B.C. to the present century, the top level shows art work since Spanish explorer days, and the natural sciences level has exhibits on botany, ecology, paleontology and geology.
MISSION SAN FRANCISCO DE ASSIS (The Dolores Mission) 16th and Dolores Sts. **San Francisco**	This is one of the oldest buildings in San Francisco, established as a mission by Father Serra in 1776. The small adobe church and tiny cemetery are better known as the Dolores Mission. The mission church withstood the earthquake of 1906 and its thick adobe walls, roof timbers and tiles are original. In the adjoining graveyard is a plaque honoring Father Palou, noted historian and biographer of Father Serra.
JOSEPHINE D. RANDALL JUNIOR MUSEUM 199 Museum Way (off Roosevelt Way) **San Francisco**	Located on a rocky promontory overlooking the city and the bay, the museum houses a main exhibit lobby, a large live animal collection, a general woodworking and metal shop, ceramics room, weaving room, lapidary and science laboratory. Young visitors are invited to study the animals and the many exhibits. Children can pet some of the animals and learn about such mysteries as earthquakes and electricity.

Westbound
passenger car toll 50¢
eastbound, free

SAN FRANCISCO —
OAKLAND BAY BRIDGE

AREA 57

Treasure Is.

ALCATRAZ ISLAND

OAKLAND

GOLDEN GATE BRIDGE

N

SAN FRANCISCO

0   4
Miles

Daily, except Mon.
10 am to 5 pm
Fri. 10 am to 10 pm

Free

10th

14th

CHILDREN'S FAIRYLAND

LAKESIDE PARK

OAKLAND MUSEUM

Lakeside Dr

N

Nimitz Frwy

17

Oak St

Lake Merritt

0   ½
Mile

AREA 57

Daily,

May 1 to Oct.
9 am to 5 pm

Rest of year
10 am to 4 pm

Adults: 25¢

GOLDEN GATE PARK

Oak

JOSEPHINE D. RANDALL JUNIOR MUSEUM

Museum Way

St

Market

17th St

MISSION SAN FRANCISCO DE ASSIS
(The Dolores Mission)

Duboce St

Delores St

Guerrero St

Valencia St

Ave

101

0   ½
Mile

AREA 57

Daily, Summer:
Mon. through Fri.
10 am to 5 pm
Sun. 12 noon to 5 pm

School term: Tues. through Sat.
10 am to 5 pm
Sun. 12 noon to 5 pm

Free

OAKLAND MORMON TEMPLE Visitors Center 4770 Lincoln Ave. **Oakland** (415) 531-1475	Standing on a hill and commanding a remarkable view of San Francisco Bay, this stately and graceful temple is a striking landmark, topped by a golden central tower 170 feet high. Guides are pleased to conduct visitors through the beautifully landscaped grounds and also the Interstake Center, a splendid example of Mormon places of public worship.
MORCOM AMPHITHEATER OF ROSES Jean St. **Oakland** (415) 658-0731	Just 5 minutes from the center of Oakland is one of the world's most beautiful municipal rose gardens. In this 8-acre setting more than 8,000 rose bushes of over 400 varieties may be seen. The garden is a pleasant combination of formal and informal displays planted on varying levels of hillside, enhanced by a waterfall and pools.
OAKLAND PARK (Lakeside Park) **Oakland**	This attractive park lies on the north shore of Lake Merritt, a salt-water tidal lake located in the center of the city. Within the park there is a special Fairyland playground for children, a wild-bird sanctuary where many species may be seen, an attractive Garden Center, a band stand and also a Japanese Garden. Adjoining is the Rotary Natural Science Center, open daily 10 am to 5 pm.
CHILDREN'S FAIRYLAND (in Oakland Park) Grand Ave. near Harrison St. **Oakland** (415) 452-2259	Many favorite characters from children's fairy stories are here to greet visitors, among them Alice in Wonderland, the Cheshire Cat, Mad Hatter, Cowardly Lion and Tin Woodman. Attractions include an Owl and Pussycat Pea-green Boat, a puppet theater, slides, mazes, a tree house and a clown. A Toonerville train ride costs 25¢ and a Magic Key to unlock all stories in Fairyland, 50¢.

Daily,

Tues. through Sat.
9 am to 9 pm

Sun. & Mon.
1 pm to 9 pm

Free guided tours

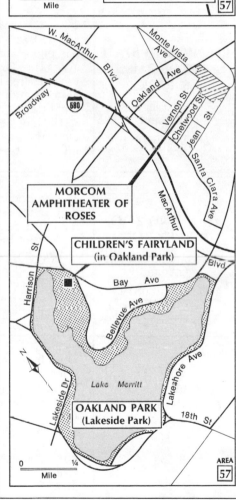

Open all year

Free

Open all year

Free

Daily, 10 am to 5:30 pm.

Spring & fall:
closed Mon. & Tues.

Winter: Sat. & Sun. only

Adults and children: 50¢

JUDAH L. MAGNES MEMORIAL MUSEUM 2911 Russell St. **Berkeley** (415) 849-2710	Artistic, historical and literary materials representing Jewish life and cultural contributions are on display in this museum, which is also a repository for historical documents and landmarks of Western Jewry. Letters, diaries, photographs and Anglo-Jewish newspapers published in the West since 1850 are among the exhibits.
KNOWLAND STATE ARBORETUM & PARK 9777 Golf Links Rd. **Oakland** (415) 568-2470	Located in southeastern Oakland, the park has picnic areas, riding, playgrounds and a zoo. The 50¢ car admission to the park includes free access to the main zoo. There is a small additional charge to the Baby Zoo and rides. The zoo is open daily, 10 am to 5 pm. Elephant shows are given on Sat. Sun. and holidays at 1 pm and 3 pm.
OAKLAND ZOO & BABY ZOO Knowland State Park **Oakland** (415) 569-8819	This modern zoo exhibits animals from many parts of the world in settings duplicating their natural habitat. An unusual attraction is the 1,250-foot-long chair lift which carries passengers high over the enclosures. In the fine Baby Zoo, children can ride a tortoise, feed sea lions, give a hippo a shower and hold, feed and touch many baby animals. It is friendly, clean and safe.
CHABOT OBSERVATORY & PLANETARIUM 4917 Mountain Blvd. **Oakland** (415) 531-4560	The Chabot Science Center is an outstanding science-math instructional facility serving elementary, junior and senior high students with special interests and ability in the areas of physics, electronics and life sciences. Special family programs include movies and presentations in the planetarium. It is advisable to telephone first for current information and reservations.

WHEN TO GO AND WHERE TO FIND IT

Daily, except Sat.
10 am to 4 pm

Free

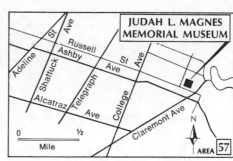

Daily,
Summer: 9 am to 5 pm
Winter: 9 am to 4 pm

Free.
Parking: 50¢ per car

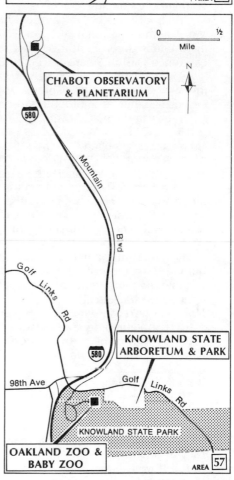

Daily, 10 am to 4:30 pm

Admission to main zoo
free

Baby Zoo: Adults: $1.00
Children 2–14 50¢
Under 2 free

Fri. & Sat.
7:30 pm to 10:30 pm
(family program)

Children's programs:
Sat. at 1 pm by appointment

Adults: 50¢
Children 25¢
Under 6 free

UNIVERSITY OF CALIFORNIA
Berkeley

The beautiful University campus is located between Hearst St. and Bancroft Way and is enhanced by many fine buildings of white granite capped with red tile roofs. Other attractive features include groves of eucalyptus trees and stately oaks, dominated by the 307-feet high Campanile (Sather Tower). Tours of the campus are offered to the general public. Other places of note that may be visited are listed below.

Tours of the Campus   (415) 642-5215

One-hour tours of the campus showing points of interest offered Monday through Friday at 1 pm. Tours start from the main lobby of the Student Union Building.

Lawrence Hall of Science, Centennial Drive   (415) 642-5132

An outstanding research center in science education containing interesting and unusual exhibits. Many of the displays are particularly fascinating and intriguing to children.

Lawrence Berkeley Laboratory, East end of Hearst Ave.
(415) 843-2740 ext. 5611

Free tours are offered to the public every Tuesday afternoon at 2 pm, excepting holidays. During the tour visitors will see a major accelerator (atom-smasher), the experimental equipment used with it and a film describing less-accessible laboratory activities. Tours last 2 hours. Cameras are permitted and visitors are advised to wear comfortable walking shoes. **Note:** *Tours are by appointment only.*

Robert H. Lowie Museum of Anthropology, Kroeber Hall
(415) 642-3681

The museum maintains exhibits on archeology, ethnology and human biology, with particular emphasis on the life-styles of unusual peoples in many parts of the world. The exhibits are frequently changed.

University Art Museum, 2626 Bancroft Way   (415) 642-1207

Both contemporary and classical art are featured in the museum together with displays of anthropological artifacts. Exhibits of the work of university students are held throughout the year. There is a film section too.

Botanical Garden, Strawberry Canyon   (415) 642-3343

The garden is located in Strawberry Canyon and covers almost 25 acres with its collection of interesting and often unusual plants, flowers and shrubs from many parts of the world. The garden is in bloom throughout most of the year and is very popular during April, May and June when the California annuals and rhododendrons are in full flower.

Campus tours: free Campanile
(Sather Tower):
Adults and Children 10¢.

Daily, 10 am to 4:30 pm
Thurs. Fri. Sat. to 9 pm
Sun. to 5 pm
Adults: $1.00
Children: 6–12 25¢
Under 6 free

Tuesday only (By appointment)
Free

Daily, except Mon. & Tues.,
11 am to 6 pm. Thurs. to 9 pm.

Daily, except Mon. & Tues.,
11 am to 6 pm.
Thurs. to 9 pm.

Daily, 9 am to 5 pm.
Free.

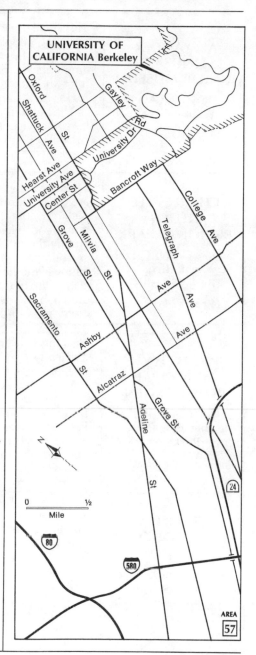

UNIVERSITY OF
CALIFORNIA Berkeley

ALEXANDER LINDSAY JUNIOR MUSEUM 1901 First Ave. **Walnut Creek** (415) 935-1978	This small museum is oriented to the interests of young people and has a varied collection of native birds and animals, as well as fish, amphibians, reptiles and other small creatures indigenous to the area. There are also rocks, fossils and shells. The animals are touchable and may be fed by young visitors. Local children can join the pet library and take animals home for a week.
CHARLES LEE TILDEN REGIONAL PARK Canyon Dr. off Grizzly Peak Blvd. **Berkeley Hills** (415) 524-1034	Outdoor activities to please almost everyone are to be found in this large, hilly park. Picnicking, golf, tennis, hiking, riding, swimming and viewing a botanic garden are among the things to do. Children will be enchanted with the Little Farm, a miniature zoo of friendly animals; also with a trout and duck pond, a train drawn by a quaint coal-burning engine, a merry-go-round and pony rides.
BERKELEY MUNICIPAL ROSE GARDEN Euclid Ave. and Bayview Pl. **Berkeley** (415) 644-6530	Visit this garden during the latter part of April and early May to enjoy the fragrant blooms of more than 4,000 roses and a view of the bay. Formerly a brushy ravine covered with poison oak, the garden was constructed as a Federal Works project between 1933 and 1937. Now it is a delightful place to stroll and admire the many beautiful flowers, including the rhododendron dell just south of the rose beds.
PACIFIC SCHOOL OF RELIGION LeConte and Scenic Aves. **Berkeley** (415) 848-0528	Founded in 1866, this is the oldest theological seminary west of the Mississippi. The small, beautiful campus contains one of the finest examples of Gothic architecture on the West Coast and a magnificent stained-glass window, dominating the Chapel of the Great Commission. The Palestine Institute Museum, located in a wing of the Administration Building, is devoted to archeology of the Holy Land, from 3500 B.C. to the Christian Era.

Daily,
except Sun. & Mon.

Tues. through Fri.
1 pm to 5 pm

Sat. 10 am to 5 pm

Free

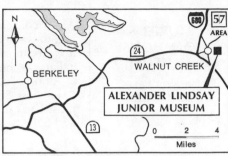

**ALEXANDER LINDSAY
JUNIOR MUSEUM**

Daily,
8 am to 8 pm in summer
Closes earlier in winter

Small charge for
swimming, rides, etc.

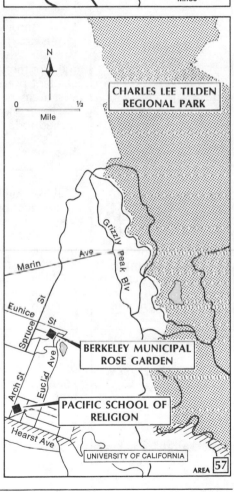

**CHARLES LEE TILDEN
REGIONAL PARK**

Daily,
during daylight hours

Free

**BERKELEY MUNICIPAL
ROSE GARDEN**

Daily,
except Sat. & Sun.
8:30 to 5 pm

(4:30 in summer)

Free

**PACIFIC SCHOOL OF
RELIGION**

MURIEL'S DOLL HOUSE MUSEUM 33 Canyon Lake Dr. **Port Costa** (415) 787-2820	An enchanting collection of rare old dolls and toys. Of historical interest are Mary Todd and Abraham Lincoln dolls and 17th-century Italian crèche dolls. Among other attractions: a painting of "The Last Supper" on a pin-head; the first music box manufactured in the United States and a 19th-century schoolroom.
JOHN MUIR NATIONAL HISTORIC SITE 4202 Alhambra Ave. **Martinez** (415) 228-8860	It was through his writings and public proposals that John Muir, the great naturalist, was directly instrumental in the establishment of the U.S. Forest Service, and the subsequent preservation of many of the West's vast areas of national parks and forests. His house was built in 1882, and is furnished today as it was when he wrote many of his articles on conservation and natural history.
DIABLO VALLEY COLLEGE MUSEUM & PLANETARIUM 321 Golf Club Rd. **Pleasant Hill** (415) 685-1230 Ext. 257	Children will find this museum interesting and educational in its wide range of exhibits. Visitors can watch a seismograph work, see a Foucault pendulum swing and then, in complete contrast, study displays of Indian anthropological exhibits. Other areas encompass oceanography and sea and shore life. Astronomy programs are given in the planetarium.
SULPHUR CREEK PARK 1801 D. St. **Hayward** (415) 581-6331	This small park and nature center gives children an opportunity to enjoy and learn about wildlife, trees, plants and shrubs. At the same time it emphasizes the necessity for conserving our natural resources for future generations. There are a well-marked nature trail, a small museum and outdoor cages where numerous small animals are on display.

Daily,
10 am to 7 pm
Closed Mon. morning

Adults: $1.00
Under 12 25¢

Daily,
8:30 am to 4:30 pm

Adults: 50¢
Children under 16 free

Mon. Wed. & Fri.
9:30 am to 4:30 pm
Sat. 1:30 pm to 5 pm

Daily,
Mon. through Fri.
1 pm to 5 pm
Sat. 10 am to 5 pm
Sun. 12 noon to 5 pm

Free

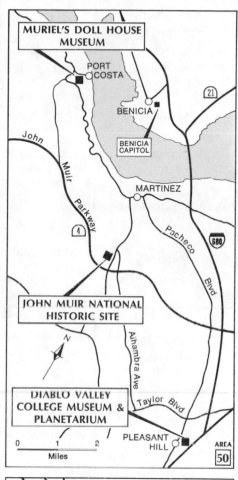

MURIEL'S DOLL HOUSE MUSEUM

PORT COSTA

BENICIA

BENICIA CAPITOL

MARTINEZ

JOHN MUIR NATIONAL HISTORIC SITE

DIABLO VALLEY COLLEGE MUSEUM & PLANETARIUM

PLEASANT HILL

0 1 2
Miles

AREA 50

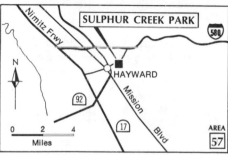

SULPHUR CREEK PARK

Nimitz Frwy

HAYWARD

92

17

Mission Blvd

580

0 2 4
Miles

AREA 57

SONOMA GASLIGHT & WESTERN RAILROAD TRAIN TOWN Broadway **Sonoma** (707) 938-3912	Set in a 10-acre railroad park, Train Town is a ¼-scale reproduction of a railroad "mountain division" of the 1890–1930 period. During the 15-minute scenic trip in open carriages pulled by a Hudson-type steam locomotive, passengers ride by a lake and then pause at the quaint little mining town of "Lakeville," also constructed to the same scale, where the puffing engine takes on water.
SONOMA STATE HISTORIC PARK Spain and 1st St. E. **Sonoma** (707) 938-4779	The park encompasses a number of structures of historical interest, including the mission, the Sonoma Barracks and the Vallejo home. Lachryma Montis was the name of General Mariano Vallejo's Sonoma home, an adobe whose outer walls were covered with boards giving the appearance of a wood cottage. Across Spain St. the Blue Wing Inn still stands as one of the earliest buildings in the pueblo.
MISSION SAN FRANCISCO SOLANO Sonoma State Historic Park Spain and 1st St. E. **Sonoma** (707) 938-4779	San Francisco Solano was founded in 1823 at a time when the general decline in the mission chain was just beginning. Settlers were encroaching on mission and Indian lands, soldiers had not been paid for years and rival politicians struggled for supremacy. The restored mission contains a noted collection of paintings of the missions of California, together with other historical artifacts and books.
BENICIA CAPITOL State Historic Park 1 & G Sts. **Benicia** (707) 745-3385	California's first state capitol building was located in Benicia and served in that capacity for a period of just one year until, on February 26, 1854, transfer was made to the new capitol at Sacramento. Today, visitors can see the building restored and furnished in the style of the period, complete with fine old desks, ledgers, whale-oil lamps and brass cuspidors.

Daily,

mid-June through
Labor day, 11 am to dusk

Rest of year,
Sat. & Sun. only

Adults: 85¢
Children 85¢
Under 2 free

Daily,
10 am to 5 pm

Adults: 25¢

Daily,
10 am to 5 pm

Adults: 25¢

Daily,
10 am to 5 pm

Free

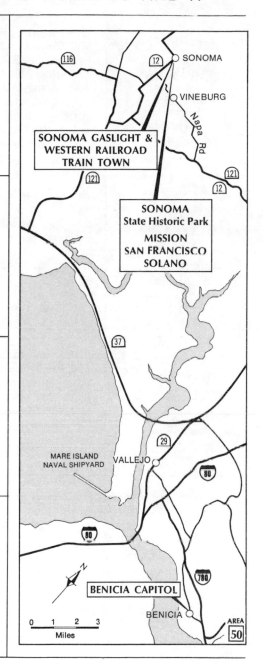

73

THE OLD BALE MILL **State** **Historic Park** 3369 N. St. Helena Hwy. **St. Helena** (707) 963-4417	This historic grist mill, known as the "Bale Mill," was erected in 1846. The first overshot wheel was 20 feet in diameter, later enlarged to 45 feet. Water was conveyed to the site from a mountain stream through redwood logs, split in two and then dug out into troughs. The last flour was ground in 1879. Today, the mill has been restored and contains early milling equipment and tools.
THE **SILVERADO** **MUSEUM** 1347 Railroad Ave. **St. Helena** (707) 963-3757	The Silverado Museum, devoted to the life and works of Robert Louis Stevenson, contains an exceptionally fine collection of exhibits pertaining to the famous Scots author. Rare first .editions, original manuscripts, autographed letters and books from Stevenson's library are among the more than 2,500 items on display. There are also original paintings, sculptures and photographs.
BAY AREA **SCALE MODEL** 2100 Bridgeway **Sausalito** (415) 332-3870	A detailed scale model of San Francisco Bay and the Sacramento-San Joaquin Delta has been constructed by the U.S. Army Corps of Engineers. Purpose of the model is to show and permit controlled study of the action of the tides and the intermixing of fresh and salt water. As the model is only in operation when an experiment is in progress, prospective visitors should telephone first.
ANGEL ISLAND **STATE PARK** San Francisco Bay	This small island park is a favorite picnic spot, enhanced by the fun of a ferry ride across the bay. Beaches for sunning (swimming is not permitted), secluded hiking trails, picnic groves and a sight-seeing bus tour are some of the attractions. See Tiburon and Angel Island Ferries (page 40) for additional details.

74

Daily,
9 am to 4:30 pm

Free

Daily,
except Mon.
12 noon to 4 pm

Free

Daily,

Mon. through Fri.
9 am to 4 pm

1st & 3rd Sats.
9 am to 4 pm

Free

All year

Adults: 25¢
Children under 12 free

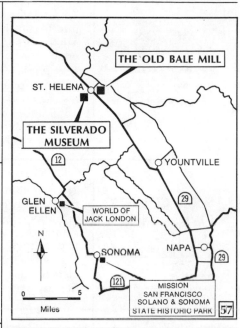

MISSION SAN RAPHAEL ARCANGEL 5th Ave. at A St. **San Raphael** (415) 456-3016	This mission was originally built as a sanitarium to aid the many Indians at the Dolores Mission in San Francisco. Chill weather and white men's diseases had been taking a severe toll. San Raphael was later raised to full status and reached peak prosperity in 1828, but by 1855 the Mission was abandoned and its decaying buildings crumbled into ruin. A replica was built on the original site in 1949.
MARIN COUNTY CIVIC CENTER San Pedro Rd. **San Raphael** (415) 479-1100	This multimillion dollar complex was designed by Frank Lloyd Wright and presents an imposing structure, housing both the Administration Building and The Hall of Justice for the county. It is open to visitors during the week, but closed to the public on weekends and holidays.
LOUISE A. BOYD MARIN MUSEUM OF SCIENCE 76 Albert Park Lane **San Raphael** (415) 454-6961	Wildlife and science exhibits pertaining to Marin County are displayed in this small museum where children will find many items that are both educational and interesting to look at. Dioramas, models, Indian tools and artifacts, stuffed animals, shells and other displays cover a wide range of local history. There is also a small gift and book shop.
MUIR WOODS NATIONAL MONUMENT Nearest town: **Mill Valley San Francisco** 17 miles	Coastal redwoods tower 200 feet and more above the shaded forest floor in this virgin stand, which includes some of the longest-lived trees on earth, many of them more than 2,000 years old. The 485-acre area was donated to the United States in honor of the famed naturalist John Muir. This park is meant essentially for hikers; there are better than 6 miles of winding trails, but no picnicking or camping sites.

WHEN TO GO AND WHERE TO FIND IT

Daily,
Mon. through Sat.
11 am to 4 pm
Sun. 10 am to 4 pm

Free

Administration Bldg.:
Mon. through Fri.
7 am to 10 pm
Sat. 9 am to 6 pm

Hall of Justice:
Mon. through Fri.
only 7 am to 6 pm

Free

Daily,
except Sun. & Mon.
10 am to 5 pm

Donation

Daily,
8 am to sunset

Adults: 50¢
Children under 16 free

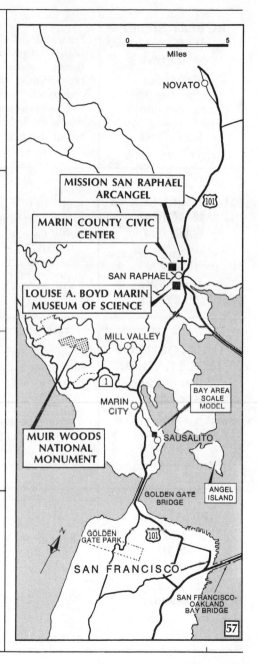

ROBERT RIPLEY MEMORIAL MUSEUM Church of One Tree in Julliard Park 490 Sonoma Ave. **Santa Rosa** (707) 528-5115	Personal articles, original drawings and a wide variety of objects belonging to the famed cartoonist are housed in this remarkable church, actually built from a single redwood. The church was featured in one of Ripley's cartoons in the *Believe It or Not* series, which he originated.
LUTHER BURBANK MEMORIAL GARDEN Santa Rosa Ave. & Tupper St. **Santa Rosa** (707) 528-5115	Santa Rosa will always be known as the home of Luther Burbank. It was here that the great naturalist engaged in his lifework, vastly enriching the welfare of mankind. In 1877 he established a nursery, which was to become world famous as the Burbank Experimental Garden. The present Memorial Gardens are dedicated to his memory and show results of some of his work.
THE WORLD OF JACK LONDON Museum and Bookstore Jack London Village 14031 Arnold Dr. **Glen Ellen** (707) 996-2888	Personal items, manuscripts, first editions, photographs, magazines, letters, scrapbooks and paintings have been collected at this museum to perpetuate the memory of the famous writer. The Jack London State Historic Park, just west of Glen Ellen, contains his grave and the remains of the author's home. Trails leading to the house and gravesite close at 4 pm.
PETALUMA ADOBE State Historic Park 3325 Adobe Rd. **Petaluma** (707) 762-4871	The adobe was the main residence and center of activity for Rancho Petaluma, the fertile, sprawling, 66,000-acre cattle ranch of General Mariano Guadalupe Vallejo. It was one of the richest estates north of San Francisco Bay. Visitors can see authentic furniture and articles of everyday use, typical of life on the great rancho. A self-guided tour leads through the kitchen, workshops, and living and servants quarters.

78

WHEN TO GO AND WHERE TO FIND IT

Daily,
May-Sept. 11 am to 5 pm.
Oct.-April 11 am to 4 pm

Adults: 50¢
Children 9–17 10¢
Under 9 free

Daily,
8:30 am to dusk

Free

Daily,
except Mon. & Tues.
11 am to 6 pm

Donation

Daily,
10 am to 5 pm

Adults: 25¢
Under 18 free

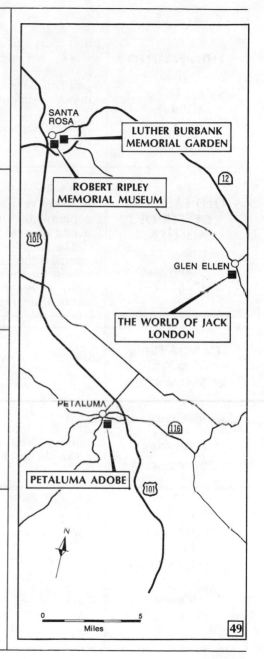

THE PETRIFIED FOREST Petrified Forest Rd. **Calistoga**	A volcanic eruption of Mt. St. Helena 6 million years ago uprooted a forest of giant redwoods, burying them in volcanic ash. Today, some of these great trees can be seen in their petrified state, turned into stone yet retaining minute detail of the origial texture and fiber. "Queen of the Forest," 80 feet long and 12 feet in diameter, is one of the astounding exhibits.
OLD FAITHFUL GEYSER OF CALIFORNIA Tubbs Lane **Calistoga** (707) 942-6463	"Old Faithful" is one of the few regularly spouting geysers in the world. It shoots forth a plume of boiling water and steam to a height of approximately 100 feet. The eruption takes place every 30 to 50 minutes; the fluctuation in the height of the plume is caused by barometric pressure, tides, moon and the tectonic stresses of the earth. The temperature of the water is 350°F.
CANOE TRIPS ON THE RUSSIAN RIVER W.C."Bob"Trowbridge 13849 Old Redwood Hwy. **Healdsburg** (707) 433-4116	One of the most popular boating rivers in the world offers 60 miles of exciting but safe canoeing through some of the most magnificent wilderness country in California. A variety of rentals are available, from 1- or 2-day trips to 4- or 5-day special trips offering reduced group rates per canoe, plus small charges for transport and camping fees.
POINT REYES NATIONAL SEASHORE Nearest town: **Olema**	Picnicking, surf fishing and the Point Reyes lighthouse are the major attractions at this seashore. Due to a constant heavy surf, the beach is too dangerous for swimming. The shore is windswept, usually cool and frequently foggy. Point Reyes national seashore is only one hour's drive from the Golden Gate bridge. Inland trails and public roads lead down to those beaches open to visitors.

80

Daily,
9 am to 6 pm in summer
9 am to 5 pm in winter
weather permitting

Adults: $1.50
Children under 10 free

Daily,
8 am to sundown

Adults: $1.00
Children 6–13 50¢
Under 6 free

Daily, Mar. through Oct.
Rentals from 8 am to 1 pm

Adults: one-day trips
$12.00 per canoe, plus 50¢ per
person for life jackets

Children over 5 free
Children under 5 not permitted.

All year

Free

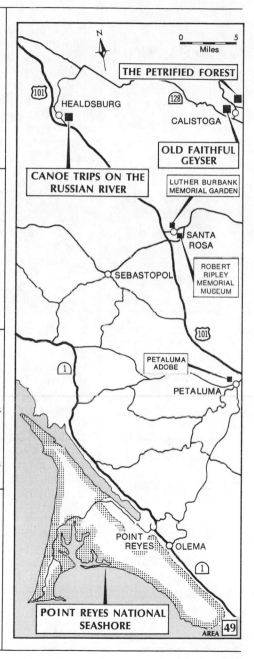

0 — 5
Miles

THE PETRIFIED FOREST

101 HEALDSBURG 128 CALISTOGA

OLD FAITHFUL
GEYSER

CANOE TRIPS ON THE
RUSSIAN RIVER

LUTHER BURBANK
MEMORIAL GARDEN

SANTA
ROSA

SEBASTOPOL

ROBERT
RIPLEY
MEMORIAL
MUSEUM

101

PETALUMA
ADOBE

1 PETALUMA

POINT
REYES OLEMA

1

POINT REYES NATIONAL
SEASHORE

AREA 49

81

CONFUSION HILL Highway 101 **Piercy** (707) 925-6456	It is difficult to disprove some of the strange happenings at Confusion Hill, where water appears to flow uphill, people seem to grow or shrink as they compare heights and walking upright becomes difficult ... for no apparent reason! The other attraction is a mountain ride through virgin redwoods where the train climbs the mountain using a unique switchback system similar to that used in the Swiss Alps.
MENDOCINO COAST BOTANICAL GARDENS 18220 N. Highway 1 **Fort Bragg** (707) 964-4352	These very beautiful and colorful acres were developed by a retired landscape nurseryman, whose love for nature resulted in a remarkable botanical garden set on the rugged Mendocino coast. Trails for easy walking wind through the natural wilderness and there are numerous picnic and rest areas and quiet scenic spots for relaxation.
THE SKUNK RAILROAD California Western Railroad **Fort Bragg** 95437	The spunky diesel and the roaring steam engine *Super Skunk* carry passengers on an exciting 40-mile trip through scenic redwood groves and high mountain passes, through 2 tunnels and over 32 trestles and bridges, crossing and recrossing the Noyo River. It is necessary to make reservations, by mail or in person, for this very popular trip. Total fare must accompany request.
FORT ROSS State Historic Park Hwy. 1 (11 miles north of **Jenner)**	Originally the American outpost for Russian fur traders of the 19th century, Fort Ross was established in 1812 when a growing scarcity of fur animals forced hunters to seek new areas for sea otter and seals. Severe damage in the 1906 earthquake and fire in 1970 have ravaged this historic cluster of wooden buildings, but excellent work has restored a unique segment of California's history.

82

WHEN TO GO AND WHERE TO FIND IT

Daily, Apr.-Sept. 9 am to 9 pm

Confusion Hill: Adults: $1.00
Children 5–12 50¢
Under 5 free

Mountain train ride:
Adults: $1.00
Children 2–12 50¢
Under 2 free

Daily,
Summer:
8:30 am to 6 pm
Winter:
8:30 am to 5 pm

Adults: $1.75
Children: 13–18 $1.25
6–12 75¢ Under 6 free

Daily, between
Fort Bragg and Willits
Call (707) 964-3798
for schedules

Adults: Round trip $8.20
One way $4.20
Children: 5–11 half-fare
Under 5 free except
when occupying a seat

Daily,
9 am to 9 pm in summer
Winter, 9 am to 5 pm

Adults: 25¢
75¢ per car for picnicking

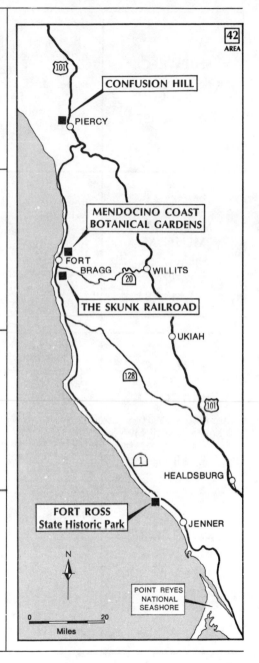

SHIPWRECK King Salmon Ave. **Eureka** (707) 442-4862	This is a replica of a 19th-century three-master. Wind-torn canvas flaps from the towering masts adding to the "shipwrecked" appearance which children will enjoy. Within the ship is a deep-sea aquarium and museum, a gift shop and snack bar. On the deck performing seals frolic in a large pool.
CLARKE MEMORIAL MUSEUM 3rd and E Sts. **Eureka** (707) 443-1947	Items of local and historical interest are exhibited in this natural history museum, including many animal heads, an extensive ornithological collection, stuffed birds and birds' eggs. Other exhibits show old guns, typewriters, sewing machines and antique dolls of American, Japanese and Chinese origin.
ALTON & PACIFIC RAILROAD Highway 36 (½ mile east of Hwy. 101) **Alton**	An opportunity to enjoy an old-fashioned steam train ride awaits visitors to the Alton & Pacific Railroad, where wood-burning locomotives take passengers on an exciting, rattling journey through beautiful country. This claims to be the only 2-foot gauge steam train ride on the Pacific Coast. Regular runs are made on the hour. Birthday parties and night runs by advance reservation.
THE SQUIRREL BUS TOURS 734 Redwood Dr. **Garberville** (707) 923-2379	This unusual sight-seeing service carries passengers through the heart of the Northern California redwoods. The full majesty of the world's tallest trees can be seen through the tinted dome of the bus, or in the open rear of the vehicle. The day-long journey includes a visit to the mill town of Scotia and a tour through the world's largest redwood mill.

Daily,
June, July & Aug.
8 am to 8 pm
Rest of year
9 am to 5 pm

Adults: $1.00
Children: 6–14 75¢
Under 6 free
Family rate: $4.50 max.

Daily,
except Sun. & Mon.

Free

Daily, except Tues.
June 15 through Labor Day
11 am to 6 pm

Adults: 75¢
Children: 1–15 50¢

Tours on Mon. Wed. & Fri.
June 17 through Sept. 6
Departs Garberville
10 am, Returns 5 pm

Adults: $5.50
Children under 12
$2.50

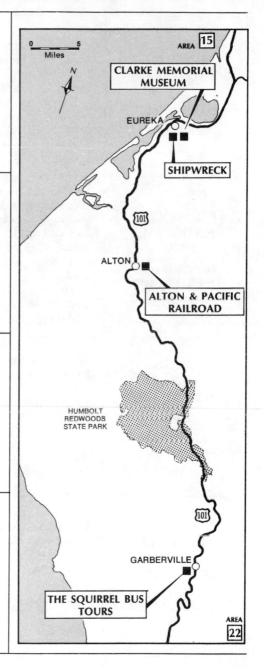

AREA 15

CLARKE MEMORIAL
MUSEUM

EUREKA

SHIPWRECK

101

ALTON

ALTON & PACIFIC
RAILROAD

HUMBOLT
REDWOODS
STATE PARK

101

GARBERVILLE

THE SQUIRREL BUS
TOURS

AREA
22

0   5
Miles

N

TREES OF MYSTERY Hwy. 101 **Klamath** (707) 482-5613	An extensive grove of redwood trees located 4 miles north of Klamath, on Highway 101. It contains a number of unique statues carved from redwood by chainsaw and made in the form of animals. Recorded commentary describes the particular features of the "Family Tree," the "Fallen Giant" and the "Cathedral Tree." There is also an Indian Museum and a gift shop.
REDWOOD NATIONAL PARK Nearest towns: **Orick, Klamath** or **Crescent City**	Thirty continuous miles of coastal acreage, plus ridges, valleys, hills and streams, lie within the boundaries of this 57,000-acre national park. Three-long-established state parks—Del Norte, Prairie Creek and Jedediah Smith—are also included within the area. This region was once dominated by magnificent redwoods, and remnants of those vast forests still remain in towering splendor.
KLAMATH RIVER JET-BOAT TRIPS **Klamath** (707) 482-2191 (707) 482-9031	Boat trips from the mouth of the famous Klamath River up through Indian country and wilderness territory provide a delightful and unusual way to explore this magnificent part of California. Deer, bear, raccoon and other animals are frequently seen in their natural habitat, and there are many opportunities for camera fans. Reservations are advisable.
HUMBOLT REDWOODS STATE PARK Ave. of Giants **Weott**	In a forest that began more than 20 million years ago, visitors will stand dwarfed beside 2,000-year-old trees, many of which reach the incredible height of more than 350 feet. The park covers more than 42,000 acres, traversed by the spectacular 33-mile long Avenue of the Giants Parkway. Magnificent redwood groves flank the south fork of the Eel river, and there are many picnic areas and campsites.

Daily,
8 am to 8 pm

Adults: $2.00
Children 6–11 $1.00

Under 6 free

All year

Free

Daily,
May 30 through Oct. 15
Departs Requa boat dock 9 am
Returns 3 pm

Adults: $8.00
Children: 4–11 $6.00
Under 4 free

All Year

$1.00 per car

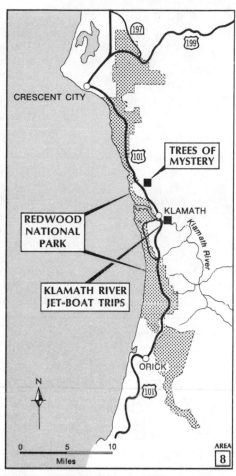

TREES OF MYSTERY

REDWOOD NATIONAL PARK

KLAMATH RIVER JET-BOAT TRIPS

CRESCENT CITY

KLAMATH

Klamath River

ORICK

N

0   5   10
Miles

AREA
8

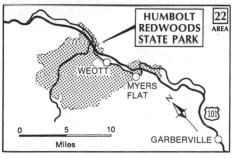

HUMBOLT REDWOODS STATE PARK

22
AREA

WEOTT

MYERS FLAT

N

GARBERVILLE

0   5   10
Miles

JOSS HOUSE State Historic Park **Weaverville** (916) 623-5284	During gold rush days a large Chinese community lived in Weaverville and erected a place of Taoist worship. In 1873 the building and most of its furnishings were destroyed by fire, and construction of a new temple was started in February 1874 on the present site. Conducted tours are given every 30 minutes during the summer and on the hour in winter.
J. J. "JAKE" JACKSON MUSEUM Main St. **Weaverville**	The museum presents the history of Trinity County from the days of the Indian through the advent of the white man, when the area became a mecca for gold seekers. Displays include Indian artifacts, mining equipment, a complete blacksmith's shop, an 1840 hand-pump fire engine shipped around the Horn, old firearms, photographs and items from the early Chinese community.
DEL NORTE COUNTY HISTORICAL SOCIETY MUSEUM 6th & H Sts. **Crescent City** (707) 464-3922	Early logging and lumber equipment is on display in this museum, together with panels of fine woods native to the area, documents, photographs and other items pertaining to pioneer days. There is also an exceptionally fine collection of Yurok and Tolowa Indian artifacts, baskets and material from the Indian shell mounds of the San Francisco area.
UNDERSEA GARDENS Citizens Dock Anchor Way **Crescent City** (707) 464-3522	Five thousand marine specimens live in underwater gardens that are 10 feet below the surface. Visitors can see many beautifully colored fish, starfish and crabs, as well as such disturbing creatures as the wolf eel and octopus. Scuba divers give demonstrations, and narration is provided by the Undersea Gardens Aquamaids. There is also a gift shop stocked with unusual and attractive items from around the world.

Daily,
10 am to 5 pm

Adults: 25¢
Children: Under 18 free

Daily,
May 1 through Nov. 30
10 am to 5 pm

Free

Daily, except Sunday
1 pm to 4 pm

Free

Daily,
April through Oct.
8:30 am to 10 pm

Adults: $1.25
Children: 12–17 $1.25
6–11 75¢
Under 6 free

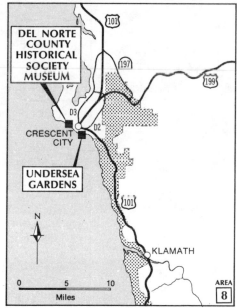

89

SHASTA DAM & POWERHOUSE Route 2 **Redding** (916) 275-1554	Keystone of California's vast Central Valley Project, this great dam holds the Sacramento River 9 miles north of Redding. Its spillway creates a waterfall 3 times higher than Niagara. The dam has made Shasta Lake, 35 miles long and with 365 miles of shore line, a recreational mecca for water skiers, boaters, campers, swimmers and fishermen.
REDDING MUSEUM & ART CENTER Caldwell Park 810 Rio Drive **Redding** (916) 243-4994	This gallery and museum features local historic displays, Indian objects and fine arts. Since the museum opened in 1963, a new fine arts exhibit has been presented every month, including oils, water colors and sculpture. There is an interesting collection of Central American pre-Columbian pottery, Mezcala stone figures and Costa Rican pottery.
LAKE SHASTA CAVERNS TOURS **O'Brien** 238-2341	Tours start with a 15-minute cruise across Lake Shasta, followed by a short bus ride 800 feet up the mountain to the location of the caverns. Well lighted and with paved walkways, the caves have striking displays of stalagmites and stalactites. Carved into a wall is the original inscription, "Discovered by J. A. Richardson Nov. 3 '78."
WHISKEYTOWN NATIONAL RECREATION AREA Nearest towns: **Shasta** or **Redding**	Located at the head of the Sacramento Valley, this new recreation area is made up of 3 large lakes and provides a wide variety of recreation for all ages. Visitors can enjoy excellent fishing, boating, water-skiing, swimming and camping. There are snack bars at the marinas, where boats and equipment may be rented and fishing gear and other items purchased.

Daily,
Memorial Day through Sept. 15
8:30 am to 8 pm

Rest of year 8:30 am to 4 pm

Self-guided tours
Free

Daily, except Mon.
Summer: 10 am to 5 pm
Winter: Tues. through Fri.
12 noon to 5 pm
Sat. & Sun. 10 am to 5 pm

Free

Daily,

May 1-Sept. 30
tours from 9 am to 5 pm

Rest of year:
tours at 10 am, 12 noon & 2 pm

Adults: $3.50
Children: 3–12 $1.75
Under 3 free

All year

Whiskeytown Lake
$1.00 per car

Clair Engle Lake
and Shasta Lake
free

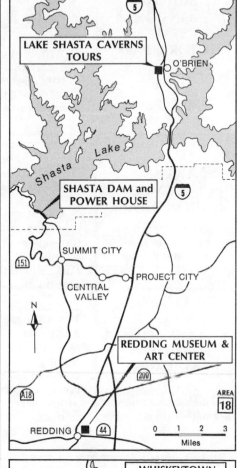

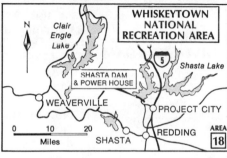

BIDWELL MANSION STATE HISTORIC PARK 525 Esplanade **Chico** (916) 345-6144	The stately mansion of General and Mrs. John Bidwell was completed in 1868, after three years of building. It was planned in anticipation of their marriage and became known throughout the West for its beauty and charm. The 26-room structure has graceful staircases, broad verandas, sparkling chandeliers, elegant furnishings and a fine library.
LASSEN VOLCANIC NATIONAL PARK Nearest towns: **Manzanita Lake** or **Mineral Lake**	At the southern tip of the Cascade range is the 10,457-foot high, plug-dome volcano, Lassen Peak, now happily dormant. The last devastating eruption occurred during 1914–15. Many active hot springs, steaming fumaroles and sulfurous vents are ever-present reminders of the volcanic nature of this region. A 30-mile road half encircles Lassen Park, and to the east there is excellent camping, hiking and skiing country.
LAVA BEDS NATIONAL MONUMENT Nearest town: **Tulelake** 30 miles **Klamath Falls** 41 miles	This strange, rugged landscape was formed many centuries ago, following the fiery eruption of a group of volcanoes that spewed fourth great rivers of molten rock. The area contains huge cinder cones, over 300 caves, collapsed tunnels and deep chasms, formed as the rivers of rock slowly cooled. The terrain provided natural defences for the Modoc Indians in their battles with the U.S. Army.
RED BLUFF DIVERSION DAM & SPAWNING FACILITY **Red Bluff** 527-7440	At this world's largest artificial salmon-spawning facility, adult salmon can be observed close up, from mid-October to mid-December. At the Red Bluff Recreation Area visitors can watch the trapping of salmon for the channels during late October to early November. The fish can also be seen on closed-circuit television as they pass through the dam.

WHEN TO GO AND WHERE TO FIND IT

Daily,
10 am to 4 pm
Tours every hour

Adults: 25¢
Children: Under 18 free

All year

$1.00 per car

All year

Free

Daily,
8 am to 4 pm

Free

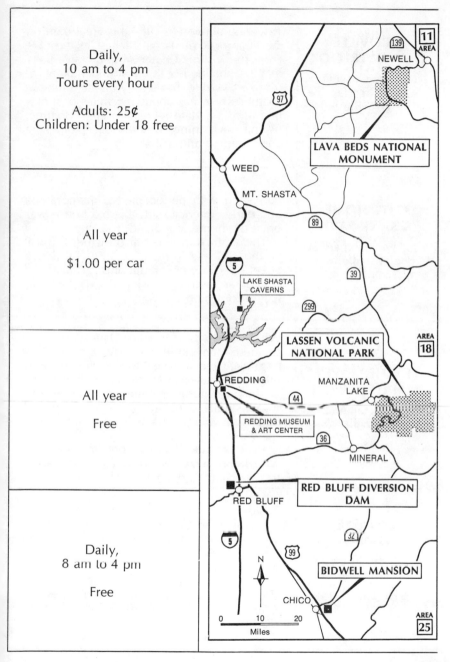

OROVILLE DAM OVERLOOK & Lake Oroville 400 Glen Dr. **Oroville** (916) 534-2409	Towering above Oroville, this great dam on the Feather River is the highest in the U.S. From the Visitors Center an impressive view may be obtained of this vast undertaking. Lake Oroville, formed by the damming of Feather River, has about 165 miles of shoreline and is a state recreation area. Boating, fishing, swimming, water-skiing, picnicking and camping are available.
LOTT HOME & SANK PARK 1067 Montgomery St. **Oroville** (916) 533-7699	Furnished with period pieces, memorabilia and early American art, this old house was once the home of Judge C. F. Lott. The admission ticket also includes a visit to the Chinese Temple at 1500 Broderick Street, a complex of Buddhist, Taoist and Confucian temples housing an excellent collection of Chinese artifacts.
FEATHER RIVER HATCHERY 5 Table Mountain Blvd. **Oroville** (916) 534-2465	When the vast Oroville Dam was constructed many miles of spawning grounds became unavailable to steelhead and salmon. To supplement the loss of those valuable and natural breeding areas, the hatchery was built so that adult fish can be moved into spawning channels or artificially spawned. Visitors may learn about the process, which ends when the young fish are returned to the river to start the life cycle over again.
CHINESE TEMPLE 1500 Broderick St. **Oroville** (916) 533-1496	Residents of the large Chinese colony that once lived in Oroville erected this temple, which is still a legitimate house of worship for followers of Buddhism, Confucianism and Taoism. The historical furnishings include gifts donated by the Emperor and Empress of China, costumes, jewelry and other *objets d'art*.

94

Visitors Center:
Daily,
8 am to 5 pm

Free

Daily,
Fri. through Tues.
10:30 am to 12 noon
and 1 pm to 4:30 pm

Wed. & Thur.
1 pm to 4:30 pm only

Adults: $1.00
Children: Under 12 free

Daily,
sunrise to sundown

Free

Daily,
Fri.–Tues. 10 am to 11:30 am
& 1 pm to 4:40 pm

Wed. & Thurs.
1 pm to 4:30 pm only

Adults: $1.00
Children: Under 12 free
(Ticket includes
admission to Lott Home)

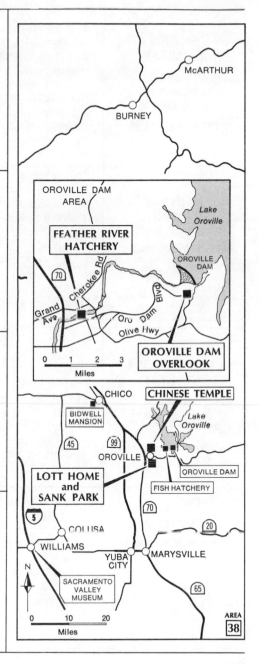

SIERRA COUNTY MUSEUM Main St. **Downieville** (916) 289-3430	This small museum was erected in the mid-1850s during the period when Downieville was the center of tremendously rich gold diggings. The town still retains traces of those early days with its narrow main street and old buildings. In the museum there are many interesting exhibits and memorabilia of this bygone era.
DONNER MEMORIAL STATE HISTORIC PARK **Truckee** (916) 587-3789	This 22-foot high memorial to the ill-fated Donner party is symbolic of the depth of the tremendous snowfall in the fateful winter of 1846, when only 47 persons survived out of the 86 who tried to cross the Sierras to California. The Emigrant Trail museum contains relics of the tragedy, which is well depicted with pictures, models and dioramas. Other items on display relate to historical features of this area.
PONDEROSA RANCH State Rte. 28, Incline Village **Lake Tahoe** (Nevada) (702) 831-0691	A re-creation of the home of the Cartwright family from television's "Bonanza" series is the principal attraction at this ranch located on the original film site at Lake Tahoe. Antique displays, the Ponderosa Museum, Penny Arcade and conducted tours are included in the general ranch admission. Horseback riding is extra.
EMERALD BAY STATE PARK Tahoma Hwy. 89 **South Lake Tahoe** (916) 541-3030	Considered to be one of the finest examples of Scandinavian architecture in the Western Hemisphere, the park's Vikingsholm is a reproduction of a Norse fortress of about A.D. 800. Built by a Swedish architect in 1928 for Mrs. Laura J. Knight, the 38-room castle was occupied until her death in 1945. The furnishings are accurate reproductions of historical Swedish pieces.

Daily,
May through Oct.
10 am to 5 pm

Free

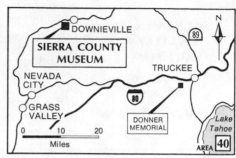

Summer, weekends:
10 am to 5 pm
Roads closed in winter

Free

Daily,
May 1 through Nov. 1
10 am to 6 pm

Adults: $3.00
Children: 4–11 $1.50
Under 4 free

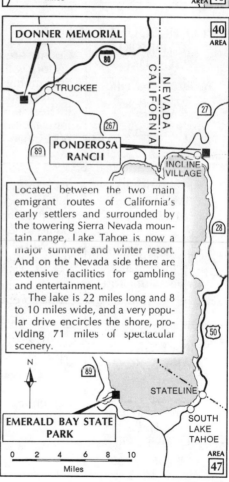

Located between the two main emigrant routes of California's early settlers and surrounded by the towering Sierra Nevada mountain range, Lake Tahoe is now a major summer and winter resort. And on the Nevada side there are extensive facilities for gambling and entertainment.

The lake is 22 miles long and 8 to 10 miles wide, and a very popular drive encircles the shore, providing 71 miles of spectacular scenery.

Daily,
July 1 through Labor Day
10 am to 4 pm
Closed rest of year

Free

SACRAMENTO VALLEY MUSEUM State Rte. 20 **Williams** (916) 473-5423	Nineteenth-century life in California is featured in this museum, which emphasizes the culture that was developed in the Sacramento Valley. Faithful reproductions of typical shops and rooms of the period include a general store, blacksmith shop, saddlery, apothecary shop, and an early home, kitchen, bedroom and parlor. There is also a display of antique farm equipment and mining tools.
PLACER COUNTY HISTORICAL MUSEUM Auburn Fairgrounds High St. **Auburn** (916) 885-9570	Early-day relics, old mining equipment and other things depicting the history of Placer County are in this small museum, providing visitors with an interesting glimpse of life in this mining town a hundred years ago. The Old Town is of considerable historic interest and contains many ancient buildings, including the firehouse, Union Bar and post office.
CALIFORNIA RAILWAY MUSEUM State Rte. 12 (between **Fairfield** & **Rio Vista**) Rio Vista Junction (707) 374-2978	The museum contains a wide variety of rolling stock acquired from many parts of the country, including the locomotive that once hauled the special train of President Taft. Young visitors will be intrigued by exhibits from earlier days and enjoy riding the cars over a 1¼-mile line traversing the grounds. There is also a gift shop and well-stocked bookstore.
MICKE GROVE PARK & ZOO 11793 N. Micke Grove Rd. (3 miles south of **Lodi** on Hwy. 55) (209) 369-2205	The park and zoo feature special gardens, picnic areas and children's playgrounds. They include a Japanese Garden, Rose Garden, Camelia Garden and Kiddieland, with a wide variety of rides. The Micke Grove swimming pool is a center of activities for the younger set. More than 500 bird specimens and 150 animal and mammal specimens are in the zoo, including lions, tigers, bears and chimpanzees.

98

Daily,
except Thurs.
10 am to 5 pm

Adults: 50¢
Children 6–15 25¢
Under 6 free

June 1 to Oct. 10
Tues.–Fri. 10 am to 4 pm
Sat. & Sun. 10 am to 5 pm

Rest of year Sat. & Sun. only

Free

Saturday, Sunday
& holidays only
12 noon to 5 pm

Museum: Free
Train rides:
Adults: $1.00
Children: 5–15 50¢
Under 5 free

Daily,

June through Sept.
7 am to 9 pm

Oct. through May
7 am to dusk
Sat. Sun. & Holidays
50¢ per car

99

OLD SACRAMENTO 1 St. South to Capitol Mall & Interstate 4 to the Sacramento River **Sacramento** (916) 447-2871	Forty-one buildings of historic interest are being restored in this old area of the city, part of a major restoration project that will bring back the golden years of river boat, stage-coach, pony express and other reminders of Sacramento's importance during the building of the West. Museums, restaurants, shops and galleries add to the charm of this 10-block area.
E. B. CROCKER ART GALLERY 216 O St. **Sacramento** (916) 446-4677	This gallery is the oldest art museum in the West and is named after Edwin Bryant Crocker, a judge of the State Supreme Court. Traveling in Europe in 1870, the judge purchased many hundreds of fine paintings and drawings. These formed the nucleus of the gallery's art collection, which today includes both modern and ancient art from throughout the world.
STATE CAPITOL 10th & 12th and L & N Sts. **Sacramento** (916) 445-2401	The golden-domed capitol building, sur-rounded by Capitol Park, is the impressive hub of political activities in the city. Com-pleted in 1874, the building is open to the public, who may watch the Senate or Assem-bly, when in session, from the visitors' galleries. The beautiful park, covering more than 40 acres, includes a collection of trees brought from Civil War battlefields.
STATE LIBRARY Library & Courts Bldg. **Sacramento** (916) 445-4374	Housed in a handsome granite building adjoining the State Capitol, the library is pri-marily a research source for state employees and the legislature. The general reading room has magnificent murals by Maynard Dixon, depicting the his-tory of California from the early Spanish days. Excellent files of past and present Cali-fornia newspapers are of particular interest.

100

Free

Daily, except Mon.
Tues. 2 pm to 10 pm
Wed. through Sun.
10 am to 5 pm

Free

Daily,
8 am to 5 pm.
Guided tours
4 times daily
Call for current times

Free

Mon. to Fri.
8 am to 5 pm

Free

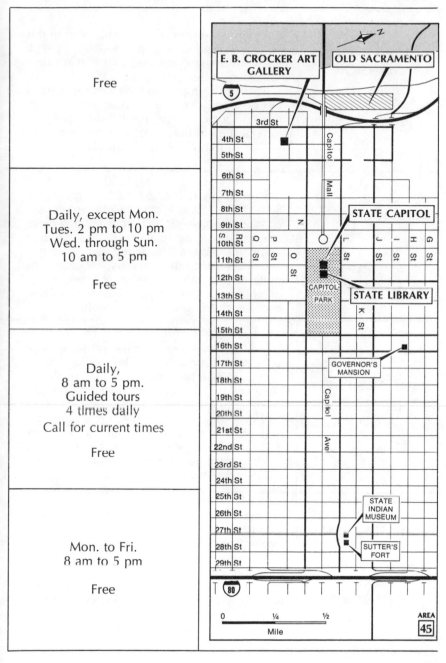

GOVERNOR'S MANSION 16th & H Sts. **Sacramento** (916) 445-4209	Thirteen governors of California lived in this official residence between 1903 and 1967. It has now been converted into a handsome Victorian Museum. The furnishings reflect the varying tastes of the occupants over a 64-year span. A conducted tour not only provides an interesting look at the old house but also covers a wide period in the history of California.
STATE INDIAN MUSEUM 2618 K Street **Sacramento**	The museum is located on the grounds of Sutter's Fort State Historical Monument and contains thousands of items ranging from articles hundreds of years old to arts and crafts made by Indians living today. Exhibits include basketry, featherwork, pottery, minerals, dress, jewelry and many other items representing some of the finest examples of California Indian culture.
SUTTER'S FORT 28th & L Sts. **Sacramento** (916) 445-4209	In 1839 John Sutter built his fort in order to preserve his surrounding Mexican land grant, and in 1844 he entertained the exploring party led by John C. Fremont and Kit Carson. Following the discovery of gold at nearby Coloma, Sacramento grew up around the fort. Now restored, the historic building contains many mementos and artifacts of those pioneering days. The State Indian Museum is also on the grounds.
WILLIAM LAND PARK 3930 West Land Park Dr. **Sacramento** (916) 447-5094	A spacious, well-laid-out park containing pools and gardens, ball parks, picnic grounds, a 9-hole golf course and an amusement center for children. In addition, there are a fine large zoo, miniature train ride, duck ponds and Fairytale Town—the last a delightful land of make-believe where the characters of fairyland are on hand to meet you.

WHEN TO GO AND WHERE TO FIND IT

Daily,
10 am to 5 pm
Last conducted tour 4:30 pm

Adults: 50¢
Children: Under 18 free

Daily 10 am to 5 pm

Free

Daily,
10 am to 5 pm

Adults: 50¢
Children:
17 and under 25¢

Daily,
8:30 am to 4:30 pm

Free

7th St
8th St
9th St
10th St · STATE CAPITOL
11th St · STATE LIBRARY
12th St
13th St · CAPITOL PARK
14th St · GOVERNOR'S MANSION
15th St
16th St

17th St — O St, P St, O St, N St, L St, K St, J St, I St, H St, G St
18th St
19th St
20th St · Capitol
21st St
22nd St
23rd St · Mall
24th St
25th St · STATE INDIAN MUSEUM
26th St
27th St
28th St · SUTTER'S FORT
29th St

80

0   ¼   ½   AREA 45
Mile

WILLIAM LAND PARK   N
Riverside Blvd
11th Ave
13th Ave
Freeport Blvd
SACRAMENTO ZOO
FAIRYTOWN TOWN
Sutterville
Sutterville Rd   AREA 45
Rd
0   ¼
Mile

103

FAIRYTALE TOWN William Land Park **Sacramento** (916) 449-5233	Initiated and maintained by the Junior League of Sacramento, Fairytale Town is a veritable children's delight, a miniature magic playground where fairy tales and nursery rhymes become reality. Exciting places to explore include Holes in the Cheese, the Rabbit's Hole, Jack and Jill Hill, Three Little Pigs and Japanese Garden. There is also a zoo with live baby animals.
SACRAMENTO ZOO 3930 W. Land Park Dr. William Land Park **Sacramento** (916) 447-5094	Situated in the William Land Park, almost 1,000 animals and reptiles inhabit this tree-shaded zoo. Among the many attractions is the island of monkeys, the ponds for otters and penguins and an excellent reptile house. The Park is beautifully landscaped with an abundance of shrubs and flowers. A combined visit to the zoo and Fairytale Town is a family favorite.
AMADOR COUNTY MUSEUM 225 Church St. **Jackson** (209) 223-0162	In this small historical museum visitors will find artifacts, gold-miners' tools and other objects depicting life in this locality as it was over 100 years ago. Other miner's and horsemen's equipment is on display in a barn and livery stable.
POLLARDVILLE GHOST TOWN 10464 Hwy. 99 **Stockton**	Many historic features of fun and interest can be found here. A tour of the main street will reveal an old firehouse with a horse-drawn pumper used in the 1906 San Francisco fire; also the smallest post office in the U.S. Be sure to visit the Silver Dollar Saloon for old-time music and refreshment.

104

Daily, except Mon.
(closed during Dec. & Jan.)
Tues.–Fri. 10 am to 6 pm
Sat. & Sun. 10 am to 7 pm
(closes earlier during
winter months)

Adults: 35¢
Children: 13–17 25¢;
3–12 15¢
Under 3 free

Daily,
Summer: 9 am to 6 pm
Winter: 9 am to 5 pm

Adults: 35¢
Children: 12–17 25¢;
6–11 15¢
Under 6 free

Daily,
except Tues.
12 to 4 pm

Free

Daily, except Mon.
12:30 pm to 6:30 pm

Sat. & Sun. only during winter

Adults: $1.25
Children 75¢
Under 5 free

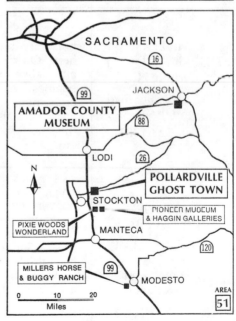

PIONEER MUSEUM & HAGGIN GALLERIES Rose St. and Pershing Ave. Victory Park **Stockton** (209) 462-4116	An extensive collection comprised mainly of 19th-century French, American and European paintings, graphics and decorative arts is on display in this 3-story building, located in Victory Park. The history collection contains items from Stockton and from San Joaquin County, arranged in interpretive display settings, including the Storefronts Gallery of 19th-century shops.
PIXIE WOODS WONDERLAND Louis Park **Stockton** (209) 466-9890	Built entirely by the people of Stockton, this delightful playground features more than 40 colorful sets illustrating fairy tales familiar to children throughout the world. There are also a miniature train, merry-go-round, numerous slides, a fire engine, rocket ship, the Pixie Woods castle, a pirate ship and other exciting things to see and do.
MILLERS HORSE & BUGGY RANCH 9425 Yosemite Blvd. **Modesto** (209) 522-1781	An extensive collection of vehicles from the horse-and-buggy days has been assembled here. On display are such items as service and delivery wagons, coaches, buggies, fire engines, early bicycles, cars and farm equipment. There is also a replica of a country store of the late 1800s, stocked with goods of that era.
SAN LUIS RESERVOIR Romero Overlook Hwy. 152 14 miles west of **Los Banos**	The great importance of adequate water supplies is visually emphasised by the many dams and reservoirs constructed throughout California for the State Water Project. The San Luis Reservoir may be viewed from the Visitor Center at the Romero Overlook, where information on the construction and capacity of this reservoir may be obtained.

Daily, except Mon.
1:30 pm to 5:30 pm

Free

Mid-June through Labor Day:
Wed.–Fri. 11 am to 6 pm
Sat. & Sun. 12 noon to 7 pm

Spring:
Wed.–Sun. 12 noon to 6 pm

Closed, Nov. 23 to Feb. 23

Adults: 25¢
Children: 1–12 15¢
Under 1 free

Daily,
daylight to dusk

Adults: 50¢
Children: 6–12 25¢
Under 6 free

Daily,
8:30 am to 4:30 pm

Free

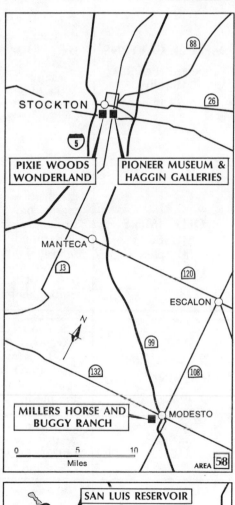

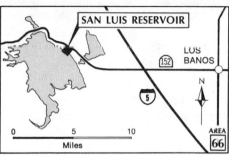

MERCER CAVERNS Sheep Ranch Rd. **Murphys** (209) 728-2101	Guided 30-minute tours are conducted through these underground caverns, which were discovered almost 100 years ago by a tired and thirsty prospector seeking water. Many beautiful crystalline formations—stalactites, stalagmites, columns and helictites are to be seen in well-lit subterranean chambers where the temperature stays at an even 55°.
OLD TIMERS MUSEUM **Murphys**	Relics of early mining days, including photographs of some of the celebrities who stayed at the old Murphys Hotel, just across the street, are on display in this museum. Reputed to be the oldest continuously operated hotel in the country, Murphys has a register that contains the names of Mark Twain, Ulysses S. Grant and J. P. Morgan among its guests.
MOANING CAVE **Vallecito** (209) 736-2708	Located in the heart of the Mother Lode, the cave was first explored by gold miners in 1851. Lowered on ropes, they warily descended into the pitch blackness, aided only by flaming torches and accompanied by the moaning of the wind. Today, visitors are conducted on a guided tour through well-illuminated rock passageways to see beautiful stalactites and, in the main chamber, human bones encased in dripstone.
ANGELS CAMP MUSEUM 753 Main St. **Angels Camp** (209) 736-2963	Relics and mementos of the gold rush will be found in this museum, where old mining equipment, wagons, carriages, tools and clothes are silent reminders of the days when Angels Camp was a roaring, vibrant gold-mining town. Minerals, rocks, gemstones and pieces of quartz containing gold are also on display.

WHEN TO GO AND WHERE TO FIND IT

Daily,
June through Sept.
9 am to 5 pm
Oct.–May & school holidays
Sat. & Sun. only
10 am to 4:30 pm

Adults: $1.75
Children: 5–11 75¢
Under 5 free

Daily,
except Mon. & Tues.
10 am to 5:30 pm, summer

Sat. & Sun. only in winter

Donation

Daily, May 15–Oct. 1
10 am to 5 pm

Rest of year closed Mon.
& Tues.

Adults: $1.50
Children: 1–11 $1.00
Under 1 free

Daily, except Tues.
Times vary

Adults: 50¢
Children:
12 and under 25¢

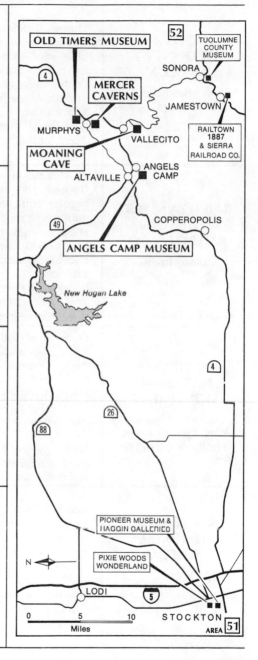

OLD TIMERS MUSEUM

52

TUOLUMNE COUNTY MUSEUM

SONORA

4

MERCER CAVERNS

JAMESTOWN

MURPHYS

RAILTOWN 1887 & SIERRA RAILROAD CO.

VALLECITO

MOANING CAVE

ANGELS CAMP

ALTAVILLE

49

COPPEROPOLIS

ANGELS CAMP MUSEUM

New Hogan Lake

4

26

88

PIONEER MUSEUM & HAGGIN GALLERIES

N

PIXIE WOODS WONDERLAND

LODI

5

STOCKTON

AREA 51

0   5   10
Miles

TUOLUMNE COUNTY MUSEUM 158 W. Bradford Ave. **Sonora** (209) 532-4212	The gold-rich area of Tuolumne county is well represented with artifacts, tools and other mementos of the famed gold-rush days. 　　Modern Sonora, busy today as it was a century ago, is a trading center for cattle and lumber. Walk half a block off the main street and you are back in the gold-rush era. Visit also the St. James Episcopal Church, built in 1860, at the north end of town.
RAILTOWN 1887 & THE SIERRA RAILROAD CO. **Jamestown** (209) 984-5686	A variety of exciting, scenic, train rides through the high Sierras is available with regular runs leaving every day during the summer months. During the winter, the schedule is restricted to weekends. Tours are also conducted through the mechanical shops, locomotives and the antique-car collection. 　　Special evening train rides, dinner rides and *"Vin et Fromage"* excursions are regularly scheduled.
PINNACLES NATIONAL MONUMENT Nearest towns: **King City** 33 miles **Hollister** 35 miles	Over a period of millions of years, rain, wind, heat and frost have combined to carve the last remnants of an ancient volcano into these spetacular crags, pinnacles and spires. Hiking trials—some easy, others strenuous—lead visitors to dramatic caverns and canyons. **Note:** *No road crosses the monument. Monument headquarters can be reached only from the east entrance.*
R. C. BAKER MEMORIAL MUSEUM 292 West Elm St. **Coalinga** (209) 935-1914	Exhibits in this museum include fossils found locally, artifacts of the first known men to inhabit the area—the Yokut Indians—and an interesting collection of Western memorabilia and photographs. 　　The extensive oil fields of the Coalinga district are represented by a comprehensive display of early drilling and operating equipment.

110

WHEN TO GO AND WHERE TO FIND IT

Summer: Daily,
Mon.–Fri. 9 am to 5 pm
Sat. & Sun. 10 am to 4 pm

Winter:
Mon.–Fri.
9:30 am to 4:40 pm

Free

Daily, May through Aug.
9:30 am to 5:30 pm
April, Sept. Oct.
weekends only,
9 am to 5:30 pm

Train rides:
Adults: $3.50
Children 5–15 $1.75
Under 5 free

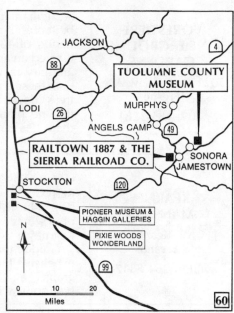

Open all year

Admission:
$1.00 per car

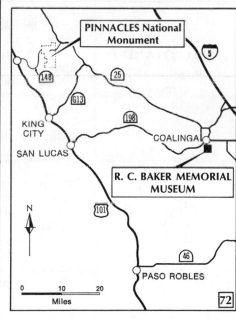

Daily,
Mon.–Fri. 9 am to 12 noon
& 1 pm to 5 pm

Sat. 11 am to 5 pm

Sun. 1 pm to 5 pm

Free

FORESTIERE UNDERGROUND GARDENS 5021 West Shaw Ave. **Fresno** (209) 485-3281	A Sicilian immigrant, Baldasare Forestiere, built this 7-acre underground estate over a period of 40 years, laboring patiently as he created an amazing network of rooms, patios and passageways. In these subterranean gardens he grew fruit trees, flowering shrubs and vines, and many that he planted still bear fruit today, more than 25 years after his death.
KEARNEY MANSION 7160 W. Kearney Blvd. **Fresno** (209) 264-8317	Home of one of the wealthiest landowners of Kern County during the late 1800s, the mansion is furnished as it was during the lifetime of its industrialist owner, M. Theodore Kearney. Guided tours show much of the house, its expensive furnishings, Tiffany lamps, photographs and other memorabilia, including bedrooms with clothes laid out.
STORYLAND Roeding Park **Fresno** (209) 264-2235	This Once-Upon-a-Time Land is proportioned to the size of children, and here they can meet major characters from their favorite story books. King Arthur's Castle, Red Riding Hood's grandmother's cottage, a Crooked Mile and Jack's Beanstalk are to be enjoyed, along with many other exciting places from the world of make-believe.
FRESNO MUSEUM OF NATURAL HISTORY 1944 N. Winery Ave. **Fresno** (209) 251-5531	This is a very good example of a small museum where the exhibits are set out in an interesting and educational manner. Dioramas of birds and animals in their natural surroundings, an extensive collection of paleontological remains—bones, fossils and skeletons—and a large exhibit of Indian artifacts make this museum of natural history well worth visiting.

112

Daily, June through Sept.
9:30 am to 5:30 pm

Oct. through May
Wed.–Sun. 9:30 am to
4:30 pm

Adults: $2.50
Children: 13–18 $1.75;
5–12 $1.00
Under 5 free

Shaw Ave

99

FORESTIERE
UNDERGROUND
GARDENS

41

Belmont Ave

Daily,
except Mon. & Tues.
March through Dec.

Adults: $1.00
Children: 6–18 25¢
Under 6 free

Rolinda Rd
Kearny Blvd
California Ave

FRESNO

Jensen Ave

N

KEARNEY MANSION

0   2
Miles

75

Daily, May through Sept.
10 am to 5 pm

Rest of year,
weekends only 10 am to 5 pm

Adults & children: 50¢
Under 3 free

STORYLAND

N. Motel Dr

Ave

W. Olive Ave

N

W

N. Palm

ROEDING PARK

Belmont Ave

0   ¼   ½
Mile

75

Daily, except Mon.
Tues.–Sat. 9 am to 5 pm
Sun. 12 noon to 5 pm

Adults: 25¢
Children: 6–17 10¢
Under 6 free

E. Clinton Ave

N

Chestnut Ave
Winery Ave

REEDY
PARK

McKinley Ave

N.   N.

FRESNO MUSEUM
OF NATURAL
HISTORY

0   ½   1
Mile

75

MARIPOSA COUNTY HISTORY CENTER 5119 Jessie St. **Mariposa** (209) 966-2924	A small museum containing a wealth of treasures. Among those that will delight the visitor are the home of explorer John Fremont, artifacts and artwork showing how gold was formed, an Indian village and a street of shops of the 1850s. Also of interest are gardens containing native trees and plants.
THE COURTHOUSE **Mariposa** (209) 966-2005	The courthouse is the oldest still in use in California, retaining many of the original furnishings. It was built 120 years ago when the town became the county seat. The 2-story building is topped by a square clock tower and contains the offices of the County Clerk and other administrative officials. There is also a fine old law library.
YOSEMITE MOUNTAIN SUGAR PINE RAILROAD Yosemite Mountain **Fish Camp** (209) 683-7273	An exciting ride on this narrow-gauge railroad carries passengers through 4 miles of scenic beauty in the high Sierras, from Yosemite Mountain to Slab Creek Loop. You may stop over at Slab Creek picnic area to enjoy a hike or a restful walk along a cool mountain stream, catching a later train for the return trip. Trains run every hour, 10 am to 4 pm, weather permitting.

SAFARI WORLD
 	
32601 Yosemite Hwy.
Coarsegold
 	
(209) 683-4474
	This wild animal ranch enables visitors to watch lions, tigers, camels, hippos, water buffalo, zebras and many other creatures in their natural habitat.
	    Tours of the compound are conducted by young game wardens using zebra-striped, wire-caged safari wagons.
	    Smaller, tame animals can be petted and fed.

Daily,
May 1 to Oct. 31
9 am to 5 pm

Nov. 1 to Apr. 30
Weekends only, same hours

Closed month of Jan.

Free

Mon. through Fri.
9 am to 5 pm

Also Sat. & Sun.
May through Sept.

Free

Daily, June 9–Sept. 9
May, Sept. & Oct.
Weekends only

Steam train, Adults: $2.50
Children: 5–15 $1.25

Railcars & Diesel:
Adults: $2.00
Children: 5–15 $1.00
Under 5 free

Daily, 9 am to 5 pm
9 am to 4 pm in winter
(weather permitting)

Adults: $2.50
Children: 3–14 $1.25
Under 3 free

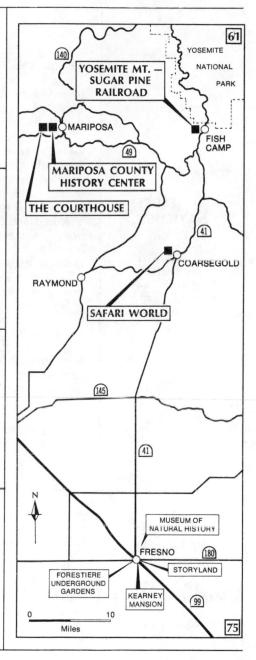

61

YOSEMITE

NATIONAL

PARK

140

YOSEMITE MT. –
SUGAR PINE
RAILROAD

MARIPOSA

FISH
CAMP

49

MARIPOSA COUNTY
HISTORY CENTER

THE COURTHOUSE

41

COARSEGOLD

RAYMOND

SAFARI WORLD

145

41

N

MUSEUM OF
NATURAL HISTORY

FRESNO

180

STORYLAND

FORESTIERE
UNDERGROUND
GARDENS

KEARNEY
MANSION

99

0   10

Miles

75

YOSEMITE NATIONAL PARK

Nearest town:
El Portal
Fresno 90 miles
Merced 80 miles

Set on the western slopes of the Sierra Nevada, Yosemite National Park is a vast region of breathtaking beauty—1,200 square miles of majestic mountains, spectacular waterfalls and lush valleys.

The major ares of the park can be explored via well-paved roads; some of the lesser-known but exceptionally beautiful areas are reached by secondary routes. Certain roads in the eastern end of the valley have now been closed to all private cars.

A free shuttle bus operates in the valley, from 7 am to 11 pm, and open tram tours leave the Ahwahnee Hotel and Yosemite Lodge at regular intervals during the summer. Fares for 2-hour tours: Adults, $3.50; children under 12, $1.50.

For fullest details of all the valley has to offer, it is recommended that visitors call first at the Visitor Center. Information about bicycling, exhibits, lectures, guided tours, horseback tours, hiking, climbing, picnicking and campgrounds is readily available. It should be noted that Yosemite Valley is particularly crowded during July and August. During winter months many roads are closed and some areas of the park are inaccessible.

DEVIL'S POSTPILE NATIONAL MONUMENT

Nearest town:
Mammoth Lakes 14 miles
Bishop 57 miles

A sheer wall of symmetrical blue-gray columns of basalt, their tops worn smooth by glacial action over millions of years, is the main feature of the park.

Rainbow Falls is a spectacular sight where the middle fork of the San Joaquin river drops 140 feet into a deep pool. It can be reached by a 2-mile hike along a trial leading from the postpile.

All year
(some access roads
closed in winter)

$3.00 per car

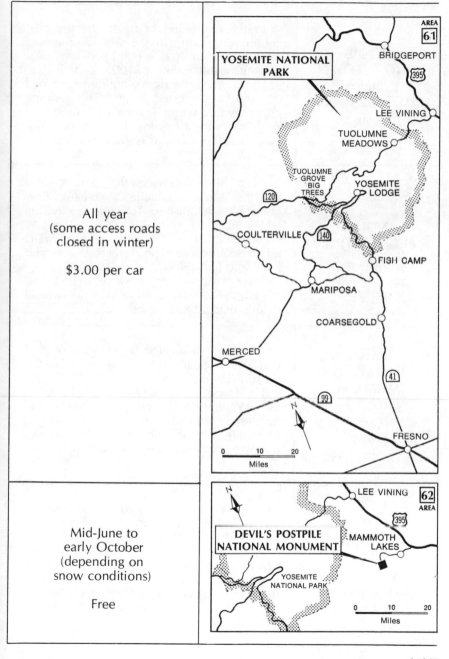

Mid-June to
early October
(depending on
snow conditions)

Free

BODIE GHOST TOWN State Historic Park Bodie	With the reputation of being the toughest gold-mining camp in the west, Bodie was once a community of 10,000 persons. Local diggings yielded almost $100 million in ore. Today, the 170 original buildings are kept in a state of "arrested decay." This genuine ghost town is worth visiting—in summer—but visitors must traverse 13 miles of washboard road to reach its isolated site.
INDIAN PETROGLYPHS Bishop	North of Bishop, between the Sierra Nevada and the White Mountains, a volcanic flow known as the Bishop Tuff forms a rolling tableland. Incised into the rocks of the area are many pictures of people, deer, insects, snakes and hand and foot prints. Their origin and age have yet to be determined; they are believed to have been made by an ancient Indian tribe.
LAWS RAILROAD MUSEUM & Historical Site Silver Canyon Rd. **Bishop** (714) 873-5950	The museum is located on 11 acres of land that was originally the railroad yards of the Carson-Colorado Railroad. The Depot, Agent's Office, Freight Room and Waiting Room contain exhibits and paintings relating to the days when Laws was an active railroad community. A 10-wheel Baldwin engine and railroad cars are also on view.
EASTERN CALIFORNIA MUSEUM 155 Grant St. **Independence** (714) 878-2010	Contains many exhibits pertaining to the history of Independence and the botany, geology and anthropology of the area. The museum was organized in 1928 in Inyo County Court House, but the early history of the town predates this by many years. Putnam's Stone Cabin was the site of the first Owens River Valley trading post, later to become Independence.

Daily,
sunup to sundown
when roads are open

(roads not cleared
of snow in winter)

Free

Daily,
10 am to 4 pm

Donation

Daily,
10 am to 5 pm

Free

62
AREA

395

BRIDGEPORT
BODIE

YOSEMITE
NATIONAL PARK

120

LEE VINING

BODIE GHOST TOWN

MAMMOTH LAKES

395

INDIAN PETROGLYPHS

DEVIL'S POSTPILE
NATIONAL MONUMENT

**LAWS RAILROAD
MUSEUM**

BISHOP

69
AREA

N

**EASTERN CALIFORNIA
MUSEUM**

180

WILSONIA

KINGS CANYON
NATIONAL PARK

198 MORRO
ROCK

INDEPENDENCE

FISH HATCHERY

THREE RIVERS

SEQUOIA
NATIONAL PARK

LONE
PINE

395

0   10   20
Miles

AREA
76

119

MOUNT WHITNEY STATE FISH HATCHERY **Independence** (714) 878-2153	The State of California maintains a fish hatchery at this location, where the study and propagation of various fresh-water fish enables the authorities to restock and supply many lakes and rivers. The Mount Whitney State Fish Hatchery is located 3 miles north of Independence.
KINGS CANYON NATIONAL PARK SEQUOIA NATIONAL PARK Nearest towns: **Three Rivers** **Pinehurst**	Here, 847,000 acres of forest and mountain wilderness are encompassed by two conjoined national parks in the southern Sierra Nevada. The northernmost park, Kings Canyon, has high mountains, glacial lakes, plunging streams and alpine meadows. Sequoia has at its eastern edge the second-highest mountain in the United States, majestic Mt. Witney towering 14,495 feet. In addition to vast reaches of high country, Sequoia contains famed groves of mighty redwoods, and it was principally to preserve the trees that the park was established in 1890. A magnificent 56-mile scenic drive, the General's Highway, links state routes 180 and 198 and provides year-round access to Sequoia. State 180, reaching into Kings Canyon, is closed by snows in winter. Lodgepole and Grant Grove Visitor Centers in Sequoia and Kings Canyon are headquarters for summer naturalist programs. The headquarters for both parks is at As Mountain on Generals Highway, 6 miles above Three Rivers on SR 198.

Daily,
8 am to 5 pm

Free

Open all year
(some roads closed in winter)

Free

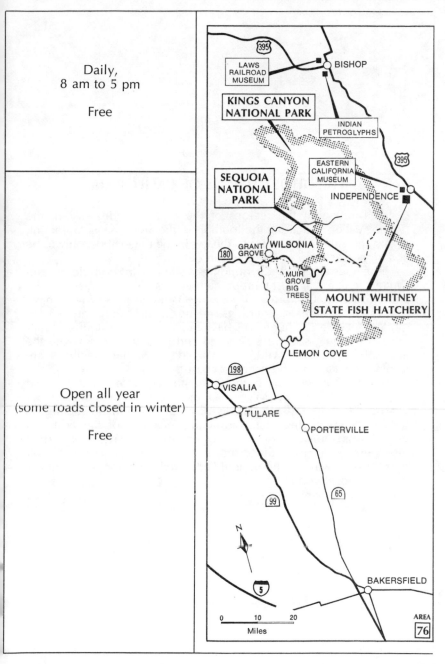

LAWS RAILROAD MUSEUM

BISHOP

KINGS CANYON NATIONAL PARK

INDIAN PETROGLYPHS

EASTERN CALIFORNIA MUSEUM

SEQUOIA NATIONAL PARK

INDEPENDENCE

GRANT GROVE   WILSONIA

MUIR GROVE BIG TREES

MOUNT WHITNEY STATE FISH HATCHERY

LEMON COVE

VISALIA

TULARE

PORTERVILLE

BAKERSFIELD

0   10   20
Miles

AREA
76

121

THE GHOST TOWNS OF CALIFORNIA

Gold! Throughout the regions of the Mother Lode, east of the Central Valley and along the foothills of the Sierra Nevada, mining towns and camps sprang up to the cry in the mid-1800s, only to be abandoned as soon as the gold ran out.

These clusters of brick buildings, often with iron doors and shutters to guard against theft of the precious gold dust, became the ghost towns of California. Today, the genuine ghost towns have few, if any, residents. Buildings are not in use and there are no modern facilities. Other towns have been turned into tourist attractions with aging structures restored and repainted to recreate the atmosphere of those wild, rollicking days. Modern facilities are available to cater to the needs of tourists.

In the far northern part of the state, the desperate search for gold continued in the area of Mt. Shasta and Weaverville and a number of more contemporary mining towns will be found in that region.

The accompanying map shows the locations of the principal genuine ghost towns, and also those towns that have been turned into tourist attractions. Since many of these places are located off the main highways, visitors should enquire locally for precise directions and local conditions.

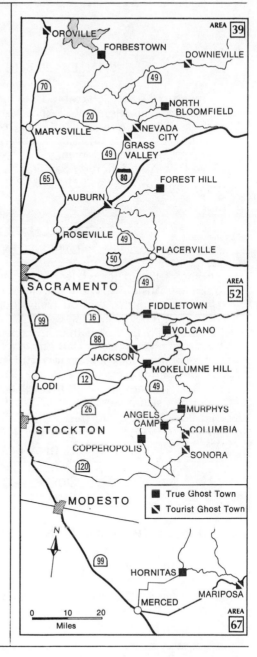

AREA 39

OROVILLE
FORBESTOWN
DOWNIEVILLE
70
49
NORTH BLOOMFIELD
20
MARYSVILLE
NEVADA CITY
49
GRASS VALLEY
65
80
FOREST HILL
AUBURN
ROSEVILLE
49
50
PLACERVILLE
SACRAMENTO
AREA 52
49
99
16
FIDDLETOWN
88
VOLCANO
JACKSON
MOKELUMNE HILL
LODI
12
49
26
MURPHYS
ANGELS CAMP
COLUMBIA
STOCKTON
COPPEROPOLIS
SONORA
120

■ True Ghost Town
◥ Tourist Ghost Town

MODESTO

N

99
HORNITAS
MARIPOSA
MERCED
AREA 67

0   10   20
Miles

123

WINTER SPORTS AREAS

Owing to the very large number of locations and the variety of facilities available, winter skiing resorts are not listed in this guide. The California Chamber of Commerce issues an excellent free *Winter Sports Guide,* covering the entire state. General skiing information may also be obtained from the Far West Ski Association (in San Francisco telephone [415] 781-2535, in Los Angeles [213] 483-8551).

SCENIC CHAIR LIFTS
Summer months only

Some of the major winter ski centers open their facilities in summer. Visitors may enjoy a spectacular and unusual ride on a ski chair lift to the top of a mountain to see magnificent views of the surrounding country.

It should be noted that, in general, the chair lifts are in operation on weekends and holidays only. As times and days of operation vary, a telephone call is advisable before starting your journey.

Three of the ski centers that will be operating their chair lifts during the summer are:

CHINA PEAK
Shaver Lake
(209) 893-3316

MAMMOTH MOUNTAIN
North Lake Tahoe
(916) 583-4211

SQUAW VALLEY U.S.A.
Mammoth Lakes
(714) 934-2571

MAMMOTH MOUNTAIN
Adults: $2.50
Children:
4–12 $1.25
Under 4 free

MAMMOTH LAKES
DEVIL'S POSTPILE
NATIONAL MONUMENT
6
395
N
BISHOP
MAMMOTH MOUNTAIN
0   10   20
Miles
AREA 62

CHINA PEAK
Adults: $2.00
Children: $1.50

N
75 AREA
CHINA PEAK
COARSEGOLD
168
SHAVER LAKE
41
0   10   20
Miles
168
CLOVIS
FRESNO   CENTERVILLE

SQUAW VALLEY U.S.A.
Adults: $3.00
Children: 2–16 $1.50
Under 2 free

80
TRUCKEE
N
SQUAW VALLEY U.S.A.
89
Lake
Tahoe
STATELINE
SOUTH
LAKE TAHOE
0   10   20
Miles
50
PLACERVILLE
AREA 40

125

THE WINERIES

Northern California has an abundance of wineries producing a great variety of premium-quality table wines.

The art of the wine maker can be explored in many of these establishments whose managements are pleased to offer conducted or self-conducted tours of their vineyards and wine-making facilities; the tours ending with an always enjoyable visit to the tasting room.

A selection of principal wineries offering tours to the public is listed on this and the following pages.

COMPANY

Fetzer Vineyards
1150 Bel Arbres Road, Redwood Valley
(707) 485-8671

Edmeades Vineyards
Philo
(707) 895-3232

Parducci Wine Cellars
501 Parducci Rd. Ukiah
(707) 462-3828

Italian Swiss Colony
Asti
(707) 894-2541

Korbel Champagne Cellars
Guerneville
(707) 887-2294

Simi Winery
Healdsburg
(707) 433-4276

TOUR INFORMATION

Daily
By appointment

Daily
By appointment

Daily
Tours on the hour
Last tour at 5 pm

Daily
Tours every 20 minutes

Daily
11:30 am, 1 pm, 2:30 pm

Daily
Tours on the hour
11 am to 4 pm

Sonoma Vineyards
Windsor
(707) 433-4403

Cuvaison, Inc.
4560 Silverado Trail, Calistoga
(707) 942-6100

Schramsberg Vineyards
Calistoga
(707) 942-4558

Charles Krug Winery
St. Helena
(707) 963-2761

The Christian Brothers
St. Helena
(707) 963-2719

Freemark Abbey Winery
3022 St. Helena Hwy., N. St. Helena
(707) 963-7105

Louis M. Martini
St. Helena
(707) 963-2736

Nichelini Vineyard
2349 Lower Chiles Valley Rd., St. Helena
(707) 963-3357

Daily
10 am to 5 pm

Daily
By appointment

Daily
By appointment

Daily
10 am to 4 pm

Daily 10 am to 4:30 pm

Daily
11 am, 1 pm, 2 pm, 3 pm,
4 pm

Daily
By appointment

Daily
Self-guided tours

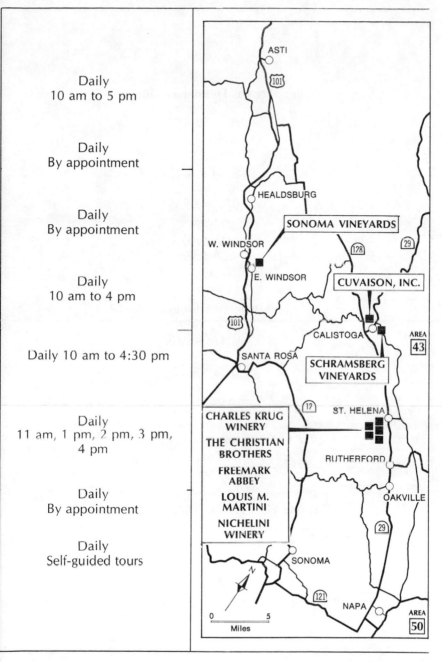

129

Beringer/Los Hermanos Vineyards
St. Helena
(707) 963-4812

Conrad Vineyard
St. Helena
(707) 963-7591

Souverain Cellars, Inc.
Rutherford
(707) 963-2759

Inglenook Vineyard
Rutherford
(707) 963-7184

Beaulieu Vineyard
Rutherford
(707) 963-3671

F. Justin Miller
8329 St. Helena Hwy, Napa
(707) 963-4252

Buena Vista Winery-Haraszthy Cellars
Old Winery Rd. Sonoma
(707) 938-8504

Sebastiani Vineyards
Sonoma
(707) 938-5532

Daily

Daily
By appointment

Daily
10 am to 3:30 pm

Daily
10 am to 4 pm

Daily
10 am to 4pm

Daily
By appointment

Daily
Self-guided tours

Daily
10 am to 4:30 pm

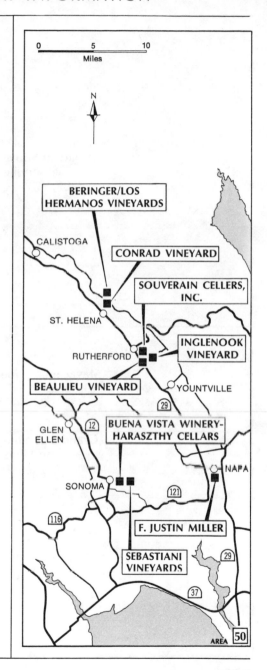

131

Chateau Souverain
Geyserville
(707) 857-3531

Mayacamas Vineyards
1155 Lokoya Rd., Napa
(707) 224-4030

Grand Cru Vineyards
Glen Ellen
(707) 996-8100

D'Agostini Winery
Shenandoah Rd., Plymouth
(209) 245-6612

TOUR INFORMATION

Daily
10 am to 4:30 pm

Daily
By appointment

Sat. & Sun. or
by appointment

Daily
By appointment

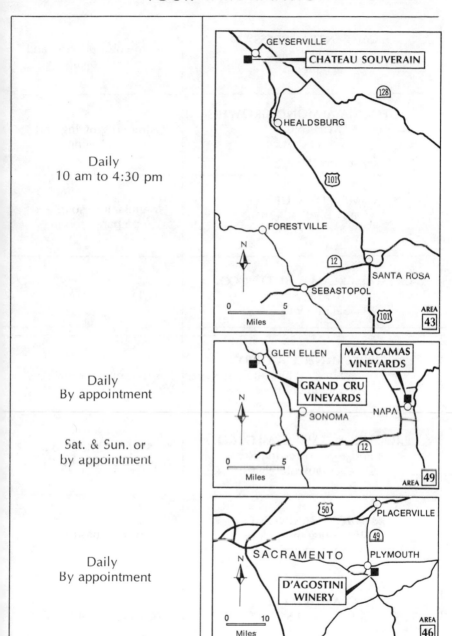

COMPANY	BUSINESS
CAL-CENTRAL PRESS 2629 Fifth St. Sacramento	Multi-color printing and periodicals
CALIFORNIA ALMOND GROWERS EXCHANGE 18th & C Sts. Sacramento	Almond growing and packaging
CAMPBELL SOUP CO. Frank Blvd. at 43rd Sacramento	Manufacture soup and prepared foods
CRYSTAL CREAM & BUTTER CO. 1013 D St. Sacramento	Dairy products
LIBBY, McNEILL & LIBBY Alhambra & Stockton Sacramento	Can manufacturing
PROCTOR & GAMBLE MFG. CO. Fruitridge & Power Inn Rds. Sacramento	Soap and detergent manufacture
RAINBOW BAKING CO. 3226 Montgomery Way Sacramento	Bakery products
SACRAMENTO *BEE* 21st & Q St. Sacramento	Newspaper publication

TELEPHONE	CHILDREN	GENERAL INFORMATION
(916) 441-5392	Yes	Mon. through Fri. 9 am to 4:30 pm
(916) 442-0771	Yes	Mon. through Fri. 10 am to 2 pm
(916) 428-7890	Yes	Mon. through Fri. 9:30 am and 1 pm
(916) 444-7200	Yes	Mon., Tues. & Thurs. 9 am to 4 pm
(916) 452-5741	Yes	Thurs. 9 am to 11 am & 1:30 pm to 3:30 pm
(916) 383-3800	Min. age 12	Mon. through Fri. 9 am to 1 pm
(916) 456-3863	Yes	Mon. Wed. Thurs. & Fri. 2 pm to 4 pm
(916) 442-5011	Min. age 7	Mon., Thurs. & Fri. 10:30 am & 1:30 pm 45-minute tour

COMPANY	BUSINESS
PETER PAUL CANDY FACTORY 1800 S. Abbott St. Salinas	Candy manufacture
McCORMICK CO. INC. Schilling Div. 1311 Schilling Pl. Salinas	Spice and seasoning manufacture
LEVI STRAUSS 250 Valencia St. San Francisco	Clothing manufacture
SAN FRANCISCO INTERNATIONAL AIRPORT San Francisco	Airport operations
ACRES OF ORCHIDS 1450 El Camino Real S. San Francisco	Commercial orchid growing
PORTERVILLE STATE HOSP. 26501 140th Ave. Porterville	Hospital operation and services
GEORGIA-PACIFIC LOGGING MUSEUM 90 W. Redwood Fort Bragg	Lumber mills and milling operation
PACIFIC GAS & ELECTRIC 1034 6th Eureka	Public utilities

TELEPHONE	CHILDREN	GENERAL INFORMATION
(408) 424-0481	Yes	Tues. & Thurs. 10 am 30-minute tour
(408) 758-2411	Yes	Tues. & Thurs. 1 pm by appointment 45-minute tour
(415) 861-4870	Yes	Wed. only, 10:30 am 45-minute tour
(415) 761-0800	Yes	Mon. through Sat. 10 am & 1 pm 90-minute tour
(415) 871-5655	Yes	Daily & Sun. 10:30 am & 1:30 pm
(209) 784-2000	Yes	Two-hour tour
(707) 964 5651	Yes	Conducted tours begin at museum
(707) 443-0821	Yes	Mon. through Fri. 8 am to 5 pm June to Sept. One-hour tour

COMPANY	BUSINESS
SIMPSON TIMBER CO. Mad River Plywood Mill Arcate	Lumber mills and milling operation
PACIFIC LUMBER CO. Scotia	Lumber mills and milling operation
MARIN FRENCH CHEESE CO. 7500 Red Hill Rd. Petaluma	Cheese manufacture
LESLIE SALT CO. 7220 Central Ave. Newark	Commercial and table salt manufacture
FRITO-LAY POTATO CHIP CO. 650 N. King Rd. San Jose	Potato-chip manufacture
LINDSAY OLIVE GROWERS 620 N. Westwood Lindsay	Olive growing and canning

TELEPHONE	CHILDREN	GENERAL INFORMATION
(707) 822-0371	Yes	Mon. through Fri. June, July & Aug. 10 am and 1:30 pm One-hour tour
(707) 764-2222	Yes	Self-conducted tours Mon. through Fri. 7:30 am to 11 am & 1 pm to 3:30 pm
(707) 762-6001	Yes	Daily 10 am to 4 pm Twenty-minute tour
(415) 797-1820	Yes	Tues., Wed. & Thurs. 10:30 am, 1 pm & 3 pm or 3:30 pm One-hour tour
(408) 251-8080	Min. age 5	Wed. only 10 am & 1 pm Thirty-minute tour
(209) 562-5121	Yes	Mon. through Fri. 9 am to 11 am & 1 pm to 4 pm Thirty-minute tour

INDEX

C

INDEX

D

E

F

INDEX

G

H

I

J

INDEX

K

L

M

INDEX

O

P

INDEX

INDEX

T

U

V

W

Y

150